Implementing Urban Design

Implementing Urban Design: Green, Civic, and Community Strategies addresses a central urban design issue: how to bring an urban design from concept to reality.

When implementation strategies are made an integral part of urban design, the result becomes more detailed, more situational, and much more likely to be related to the natural landscape and the character already present in the community. The strategies described in this book range from neighborhoods to downtown business districts, and from designs for whole suburbs and cities to designs at the scale of the region and megaregion. They deal with everyday situations, although some of the issues can be complicated.

This book will interest community leaders, urban design professionals, and the students, instructors, and practitioners of urban design and city planning.

Jonathan Barnett has been an urban design advisor to the cities of Charleston, SC, Cleveland, Kansas City, Miami, Nashville, New York City, Norfolk, Omaha, and Pittsburgh in the United States and Xiamen and Tianjin in China. He has also advised the U.S. Department of Housing and Urban Development, the National Park Service, the National Endowment for the Arts, and the National Capital Planning Commission. He is the author of many books and articles about urban design and planning and is a professor emeritus of practice in city and regional planning at the University of Pennsylvania.

Implementing Urban Design
Green, Civic, and Community Strategies

Jonathan Barnett

NEW YORK AND LONDON

Designed cover image: Areas of Civic Importance in Omaha, Nebraska. Drawing by Yan Wang, courtesy of WRT

First published 2023
by Routledge
605 Third Avenue, New York, NY 10158

and by Routledge
4 Park Square, Milton Park, Abingdon, Oxon, OX14 4RN

Routledge is an imprint of the Taylor & Francis Group, an informa business

© 2023 Jonathan Barnett

The right of Jonathan Barnett to be identified as author of this work has been asserted in accordance with sections 77 and 78 of the Copyright, Designs and Patents Act 1988.

All rights reserved. No part of this book may be reprinted or reproduced or utilised in any form or by any electronic, mechanical, or other means, now known or hereafter invented, including photocopying and recording, or in any information storage or retrieval system, without permission in writing from the publishers.

Trademark notice: Product or corporate names may be trademarks or registered trademarks, and are used only for identification and explanation without intent to infringe.

Library of Congress Cataloging-in-Publication Data
Names: Barnett, Jonathan, author.
Title: Implementing urban design : green, civic, and community strategies / Jonathan Barnett.
Description: New York : Routledge, 2023. | Includes bibliographical references and index.
Identifiers: LCCN 2022061313 (print) | LCCN 2022061314 (ebook) | ISBN 9781032469942 (hardback) | ISBN 9781032469966 (paperback) | ISBN 9781003384106 (ebook)
Subjects: LCSH: City planning--Environmental aspects. | Community development. | Landscape architecture. | Regional planning.
Classification: LCC HT166 .B3734 2023 (print) | LCC HT166 (ebook) | DDC 307.1/216--dc23/eng/20230223
LC record available at https://lccn.loc.gov/2022061313
LC ebook record available at https://lccn.loc.gov/2022061314

ISBN: 9781032469942 (hbk)
ISBN: 9781032469966 (pbk)
ISBN: 9781003384106 (ebk)

DOI: 10.4324/9781003384106

Typeset in Corbel
by KnowledgeWorks Global Ltd.

Also by Jonathan Barnett, *City Design: Modernist, Traditional, Green and Systems Perspectives*, 2nd edition, Routledge 2016

Contents

Introduction: Implementing Urban Design	1
1. Including the Community in Design Decisions	3
2. Protecting the Environment	19
3. Designing Cities Without Designing Buildings	34
4. Enhancing Public Open Spaces	52
5. Preserving Existing Urban Designs	65
6. Changing Regulations to Prevent Suburban Sprawl	79
7. Reinventing Suburban Development	93
8. Using Bus Rapid Transit in Suburbs	105
9. Mobilizing Support to Redesign an Entire City	118
10. Designing for Regions and Megaregions	133
Afterword: Imp ementing Urban Design for a Changing World	147
Suggestions for Additional Reading	149
Illustration Crecits	153
Notes	156
Index	160

INTRODUCTION: IMPLEMENTING URBAN DESIGN

Bringing an urban design concept to its real-world completion is a complicated interactive process. There are many available illustrations of urban design concepts, and many photos of completed projects, but not much has been published about what happens in between. Today's cities and suburbs are shaped by decisions made by powerful and often competing forces: by the real-estate development industry, by government investment and regulations, as well as by communities, which, although represented by government, can organize to defend their immediate interests, which are not always the same as government objectives.

Preparing an urban design that will draw the support of all the interest groups that will have to agree to implementation requires the designer to understand as much as possible about landscapes and natural systems, the needs of all the people who live and work in cities and suburbs, the functional parts of urban places and their relationships, the economic conditions that drive real-estate investment, the role that public funding can play, and the regulations by which public policy can influence private financial decisions.

As no one is equally proficient in all these areas, urban design is usually the work of a team with different specialties, but it is the designer who should lead the team because design is a methodology for resolving potential conflicts.

Anyone who has ever arranged or rearranged furniture in a room has become conversant with the essence of the design process, which requires resolving a problem of inter-related variables by proposing alternative configurations and assessing their advantages and disadvantages. It can save a lot of effort to sketch out and evaluate some of the potential variations before moving the furniture around.

A comparable process can apply to the design of a house where structure and economics are added to the variables, or a garden which will require an understanding of plants and natural systems. A comparable, but more complex methodology is used for a large building or a park, or a campus of buildings and open spaces. The same methods can be used for planning whole districts, for new communities, and for guiding the development of regions and megaregions.

DOI: 10.4324/9781003384106-1

As urban design plans usually rely for all or part of their implementation on the private real-estate market or the backing of major institutions, a successful urban design proposal must be seen to be a sound investment. Government intervention is usually required to make a development happen, so urban designers should demonstrate which interventions can produce the most desirable design outcomes, and how regulation can be a more positive force in guiding development. Design can improve the public discussion of development proposals by helping people visualize and choose which alternate future they prefer, and then show how buildings, streets, and public open space can fit together to form attractive places. But these designs must also make financial sense both for investors and for governments allocating their limited resources.

The following chapters contain examples, implemented in a range of cities and suburbs across the United States, which are drawn from my experience as an urban design consultant. They provide an inside story of how the design originated, how each was implemented, and what has happened since. Some of the illustrations are high-resolution photographs from Google's satellite and street-view imagery, so you can decide for yourself how successful each design has been. You are also sometimes referred to legislation that has turned a design into statutory requirements.

These urban designs are supported by three categories of strategies: Green, preserving the natural environment and dealing with a changing climate; Civic, protecting the public interest in both private and publicly funded investments; and Community, which not only means bringing communities into the process where design and development decisions are made but also includes using walkable neighborhoods to give structure to cities and suburbs.

1

INCLUDING THE COMMUNITY IN DESIGN DECISIONS

Consulting with the people most affected by a development was once a radical, untried idea. A public hearing was required for important government actions, but by then, it was far too late to show a community a plan for its future. It was like an architect waiting to show a house design to the client until all the drawings are done and it is time to ask contractors for bids. However, urban renewal in U.S. cities went forward without consulting communities until a combination of public pressure and failed projects brought change. Including community concerns in planning and design decisions is necessary not only to reach an equitable result but as a way of avoiding, or at least reducing, expensive and time-consuming controversies about new development. It is also a way to learn from local residents and business people about the real conditions in their area. Making the public part of the design process then changes the designs. They became much more fine-grained, more situational, much less likely to be a grand vision, and much more likely to be based on the design character already present in the community.

I was part of an early experiment in community-based urban design which turned out to have been influential in establishing it as essential. I have continued to develop community-based urban designs ever since. The early experiment began when I and four colleagues, Giovanni Pasanella, Jaquelin Robertson, Richard Weinstein, and Myles Weintraub, were volunteer policy advisors during John Lindsay's 1965 campaign for mayor of New York City.

We prepared several of the campaign's position papers, including one advocating changes in the way the city managed urban renewal in neighborhoods officially found to be blighted. City staff had been making observations of dilapidation and deterioration, often based on no more than a windshield survey (driving through the neighborhood) or a mailbox survey (checking the names on mailboxes within each building to see if there was overcrowding). This kind of evidence was used to make an official finding of blight. Then, almost every property within the boundaries established by the finding would be acquired by the city, the residents and businesses moved out, and the buildings torn down. A renewal plan would be developed for a completely new group of buildings separated by green areas. In New York, these policies were associated with Robert Moses, who had set the direction for urban renewal for decades. By 1965, Moses was no longer in charge but the same process was still going on.

DOI: 10.4324/9781003384106-2

Similar procedures had been followed in many other cities, backed by federal money under the Housing Act of 1954.

We wrote that this kind of wholesale demolition was wrong not only for its devastating effect on the people who were displaced but also because no one involved in the decision had enough information to make these judgments, and this kind of major surgery was rarely necessary. We proposed that the acquisition of building sites should be far more selective, the new buildings should be designed to fit into the existing urban context, and the people who lived in the neighborhood, who were the real experts about what was happening, should be involved in making the planning decisions.

After Lindsay won the election, we all went back to our day jobs. Gio, Jaque, Richard, and Myles were all working for a well-known architect, Edward Larrabee Barnes. I had worked for Haines Lundberg and Waehler (HLW), a large architectural office, and was then an editor at the *Architectural Record*. It had not occurred to us to want to work for the city, where most of the jobs for architects were about reviewing plans for the building department.

Donald Elliott had run the part of the campaign that developed the speeches and position papers. He was a close associate of Lindsay, and when Lindsay took office, Don became the Counsel to the Mayor, and Lindsay put him in charge of staffing the top jobs in the city agencies. Don reserved for himself becoming the Chair of the Planning Commission, which, in New York City, meant he would also be the Director of the planning department. Don Elliott decided to have the five of us who had written his position papers about urban design try out our strategies in a real situation. He helped us obtain a grant from the J. M. Kaplan Fund to prepare a prototype housing and urban design plan.

Community-based urban renewal in the Bronx

Elliott chose the Twin Parks district which consisted of several different neighborhoods in New York City's borough of the Bronx and made sure that it had an allocation of government financing for new middle-income and public housing. We would select the redevelopment sites to minimize the disruption from city acquisitions. The community would review our proposals in public meetings as we prepared the plan – for New York at that time a new and long overdue approach. Giovanni Pasanella had started his own firm in a studio at Carnegie Hall, and we did the work there. The community meetings were mostly at night. I didn't go to the initial presentation to the community because I was traveling for the *Record* and was spared experiencing the overwhelmingly hostile reception. People refused to believe that our slides of deteriorated buildings and vacant lots strewn with rubbish had been taken in their communities, and they didn't want to talk about any kind of new housing.

I had just written an article for the *Record* about a successful downtown plan in Cincinnati.[1] Archibald Rogers, an architect from Baltimore, had been called in after several failed attempts by the Cincinnati City Council to agree on a plan. Rogers had outlined a new, four-stage process. First, reconnaissance and research, then an identification of potential objectives. Third, the selection of objectives that everyone could agree were necessary, and, finally, agreement about tactics: decisions about what to do and where and when to do it. At each of the stages, an advisory committee voted, and their decision went to the City Council which reviewed and approved each step in the form of ordinances. When the plan was completed, its approval was already built in.

I realized that we had skipped the first phase of a Cincinnati process, agreement about the actual situations in the Twin Parks area. Gradually, in smaller meetings, we established working relationships and some confidence that what we were doing was intended to be helpful. Father Mario Zicarelli of the Church of Our Lady of Mount Carmel in the Belmont neighborhood in Twin Parks was an important intermediary for us and introduced us to leading figures in other Twin Parks neighborhoods. This time around, we were careful to start by reaching agreement about actual conditions. Our ground rules specified that there would be no investment in private (but subsidized), middle-income housing unless there was also an increment of public low-income housing, but we could discuss different ways to deploy these city resources. We located potential development sites that were either vacant land or occupied mainly by small commercial or industrial structures, so no people would have to move out of their homes. We chose sites to be parts of coordinated designs for two locations: the western edge of the Twin Parks district where it met the higher ground of University Heights and, on the east, along the edge of Bronx Park. Our strategy of strengthening the edges of the community would be backed up by programs for enforcing the building code and providing grants to rehabilitate existing buildings across the whole area.

When the sites for both kinds of new housing were finally worked out after many meetings, people who had participated in discussions about the plan were willing to speak in favor of it at the two community planning boards that shared jurisdiction over the area and at the public hearing at City Hall so that the plan ended up being adopted as city policy without any public controversy. Our planning process was nowhere near as structured as what Rogers had organized in Cincinnati, but it demonstrated it was possible for the city to work constructively with communities and showed how important it is to give them a voice.

Donald Elliott and Eugenia Flatow were in overall charge of New York City's Model Cities Program, a federally supported community investment program which was passed by Congress in 1966 and began in the South Bronx, Harlem, and Central Brooklyn when we were already at work in Twin Parks. Don and Gene made sure that the Model Cities plans would be prepared with comparable community involvement and that the same policies of selective rebuilding on vacant housing sites or underused industrial properties, plus code enforcement and rehabilitation grants, would also be followed. The policies tested in Twin Parks would also replace total clearance for all other urban renewal projects in New York City, and the participation of local communities would continue to be essential in identifying the places where city investment would be most effective.

Our work in Twin Parks was being done at a low point of conditions in the Bronx. Large numbers of people were moving out, many buildings were being abandoned, and often later destroyed by fire. Crime rates were way up. When I thanked Father Zicarelli for all the time he was spending with us, he said: "Jonathan, when a man is drowning, he will reach for a spar; and, if there is no spar, he will clutch at a straw."

The Twin Parks plan was implemented through an agreement between New York City and the New York State Urban Development Corporation (UDC), then directed by Edward Logue, well-known for his work on urban renewal in New Haven and Boston. The UDC, seeing that the

1.1 This photo shows the western edge of the Twin Parks district at the time we began our meetings with the community in 1966. Tiebout Avenue in the University Heights neighborhood at the top of the stairs was in relatively good shape but showing its age. At the foot of the rock escarpment were small structures in an industrial zone along Webster Avenue, an important traffic artery. Many of these buildings were empty. We saw the land at the foot of the stairs as an opportunity to build some ten-story buildings at the lower level, with their upper floors still being in scale with the development along Tiebout Avenue, which was mostly four and five stories.

locations we had selected were complicated, and not at all like the usual urban renewal sites where large areas had been completely cleared away, selected innovative architects who could realize the kinds of buildings we had drawn in our plans, including Giovanni Pasanella, James Polshek, Richard Meier, and Prentice Chan Ohlhausen.

We had understood that a community-based urban design had to be situational, and we looked for opportunities within the existing structure of each neighborhood. On our initial visits, I had been attracted by land next to a rock escarpment with a long flight of stairs linking the University Heights neighborhood above to the Twin Parks area below, where there was a scattering of small industrial buildings along Webster Avenue, many of them unoccupied. There was room for any business that would have to move because of our plans (1.1).

INCLUDING THE COMMUNITY IN DESIGN DECISIONS

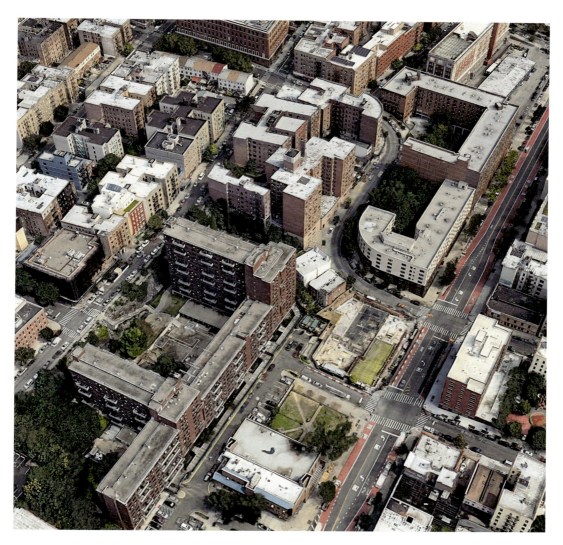

1.2 The area shown in 1.1 as it looked in 2022. Tiebout Avenue is on the left, Webster Avenue on the right. The long building with two attached wings in the foreground is housing managed by the New York City Housing Authority. The architect was Giovanni Pasanella. The building with the courtyard in the top right-hand part of the photo is subsidized middle-income housing designed by Prentice Chan Ohlhausen. These buildings, now about 50 years old, were designed to fit into irregular sites with as little disturbance to other existing development as possible, as opposed to what was then the standard practice of building separate tall towers on cleared land. These investments have encouraged incremental improvements to the surrounding buildings, strengthening the whole neighborhood just as we intended.

Here was a place where the upper floors of a relatively tall building constructed at the lower level near a main street could fit well into the mid-rise context of Tiebout Avenue up at the top of the stairs. Sites along this escarpment became places where we could make substantial changes without disturbing well-constructed existing buildings, which were either still in sound condition or could be repaired and continue to have a useful life. This photo from Google Earth (1.2)

1.3 On the eastern side of Twin Parks, we understood the frontages along Southern Boulevard facing Bronx Park, home of the famous Bronx Zoo, to be under-appreciated locations where taller buildings would not disrupt the neighborhood. The lower left-hand side of the photo shows two residential towers turned to form a gateway to Easy 187th Street, a main street of the Belmont neighborhood. At the top of the photo is another group of apartments with a tower that marks the north-east corner of the Belmont neighborhood. Both sets of buildings were designed by Giovanni Pasanella.

1.4 Another subsidized middle-income apartment building from our plan, also facing Bronx Park across Southern Boulevard, wraps around a small apartment building and three houses on Southern Boulevard and two more small apartment buildings and two more houses around the block on Grote Street. It was highly unusual when this building was designed to select a block for government-subsidized housing where a substantial part of the existing development was left intact. The architect for the new buildings was Richard Meier.

shows some of the new development we planned along the divide between University Heights and Webster Avenue as it looked in 2022. The buildings in the foreground are public housing designed by Giovanni Pasanella; the building with the large courtyard at the top of the photo contains middle-income apartments designed by Prentice Chan Ohlhausen.

Across Twin Parks, among the blocks we selected along Bronx Park, two sites across from each other on 187th Street were an opportunity to create a symbolic gateway into the heart of the Belmont neighborhood and

to place an apartment tower marking the north-east corner of the neighborhood at Fordham Road. Both sets of buildings were also designed by Giovanni Pasanella (1.3). The urban design expectations in the plan were fulfilled by the new buildings, but they fit so closely into the existing context that they don't read as a separate urban design, as shown by this building, also in Twin Parks East, designed by Richard Meier which wraps around the previously existing buildings located on the rest of the block. An infill site like this one was highly unusual for new public development at the time (1.4). These neighborhoods today have been preserved and reinforced, exactly as we intended.

As we finished our work in Twin Parks, Don Elliott persuaded Jaque, Richard, Myles, and I to come to work for him at the City Planning Department. I have written about our experiences there in *Urban Design as Public Policy: Practical Methods for Improving Cities,* published in 1974,[2] and will also use some examples in Chapters 2 and 3 of this book to show how projects designed while we were working for the city have since been completed.

How community involvement in planning and design has developed

Simply making presentations to the community while planning was in progress, and learning from the reactions, was definitely a step forward in 1965, but today communities expect to be more closely involved with the whole design and planning process.

Advocacy and Pluralism in Planning: At about the same time that we were writing our position papers for John Lindsay's campaign, Paul Davidoff was publishing an influential article in what was then called the *Journal of the American Institute of Planners* arguing that communities should have advocates who would help them draw up their own plans to counter those being made by people in authority. These advocacy planners would help communities to have an equal voice in decisions about their future.[3]

In contrast to our mediating role in Twin Parks, where we were working for the city but made plans we intended to help the community, Davidoff, a lawyer, thought that the right course of action always needed an adversarial process. The difficulty with his formulation was that there was no analogy to a judge or jury in the process of making changes in cities. Faced with plural plans, who would decide what to do? Another problem was that the communities most in need of advocacy could least afford to pay an advocate, especially as any community-based planning process requires an extended period of consultation and review.

The concept of advocacy planning appealed for a time to young architects who volunteered their services to help communities. But working with communities turned out to be long, difficult, and worse than thankless, as there was a lot of – justified – anger in many communities, and people wondered who these outsiders were and what they were up to. An unfortunate result was that many of these architects gave up on the whole idea of urban design and retreated into conventional architectural practice.

What made a form of advocacy work were university-based centers for community development. One of the first was founded in 1963 by Ronald Schiffman at Pratt Institute in Brooklyn. Today, there are many others, which form a national network of university-based community development centers. These non-profit centers provide funding for some designers and planners, usually also faculty members, who can draw on other professors and students, creating a valuable bridge between theory and practice while offering professional services to communities.

These university-based centers have helped support community development corporations. A model was the Bedford Stuyvesant Renewal and Rehabilitation Corporation, established in the mid-1960s with the patronage of Senator Robert Kennedy and with support from the Pratt Center for Community Development. Community-based development is now well-established, a partial answer to the question posed by Paul Davidoff about who would advocate for communities, although there is still no judge – unless a plan ends up in court.

When the Community Says No: When the National Park Service planning team presented their proposed General Management Plan for the Gateway National Recreation Area in New York City and New Jersey in 1974, they ran into acrimonious opposition from the communities bordering the proposed park. These communities were well-organized and turned out many angry people for meetings. They didn't need any other advocates.

The Regional Plan Association had proposed in 1969 that publicly owned coastal areas of the New York City region should be designated a National Seashore. The idea had the support of Mayor Lindsay and of Walter Hickel, then the Secretary of the Interior. Although President Nixon fired Hickel in 1970, the idea of a shoreline park in the New York–New Jersey metropolitan area continued to be supported by the Nixon administration. Donald Elliott, as the Planning Commission chair, represented New York City in negotiations with the federal government about creating the new parkland. In 1972, Congress passed legislation creating the first two urban national parks, the Gateway National Recreation Area in the New York City region and the Golden Gate National Recreation Area in San Francisco.

When opposition to the Gateway plans developed, Marian Heiskell, an influential public figure who had led the campaign to establish Gateway (she was part of the family that owned *The New York Times* and her husband was the chairman of Time Incorporated), recommended that the Park Service consult Donald Elliott about what to do next. Donald had gone back to his law firm, Webster & Sheffield, in 1973. Donald suggested that the Park Service retain me and my urban design group colleague Richard Weinstein to help them guide their plan through to public approval. Lindsay had just left office and Richard, who had become the director of the Office of Lower Manhattan Development, had left the city government and was establishing himself as a consultant.

Richard and I met with the Park Service planners in their temporary offices at Floyd Bennett Field in Brooklyn and found them to be a highly competent group. We listened to their presentation and didn't think anything much was wrong with their plans. We explained that

New Yorkers had learned to project their worst fears on to any proposed new development and had very frequently been right in the past. What the Park Service needed to do was deconstruct what they had already done and put it back together as part of a public involvement process. We went through what we thought was needed: a listening and fact-finding stage, a discussion of alternatives, decisions – which we thought it likely would be similar to conclusions they had already reached, and then, and only then, the presentation of the final plans.

Dwight Rettie, who was a special assistant to the director of the National Park Service, had been designated to sort out what was happening at Gateway. He approved the direction we suggested and made sure that the staff was authorized to spend the necessary time. The Park Service retained Richard and me as per-diem consultants. Richard found that, at the Park Service rates, he couldn't afford to devote much of his time to Gateway. He did contribute good ideas to some in-house design and planning sessions. I was by this time a professor at the City College directing their Graduate Program in Urban Design. The College permitted me to do some consulting, and I did not have to worry about the compensation.

Michael Adlerstein, who was in charge of the Gateway team for the Park Service, was quite capable of managing the public involvement process.[4] He didn't need much help, and, of course, I was also teaching and involved in other work.

One of the big reasons for the public protests was the future of the private beach clubs along the Rockaway Peninsula, next to the public beaches at Riis Park. These clubs had been leasing their beachfront land from the city, and, when ownership was transferred from the city to the Park Service, the Park Service thought that the clubs should be removed and their beaches made accessible to the public – in keeping with Park Service practice. The Park Service had had no idea how important these clubs were for many people. When they understood the issue, they offered a compromise: the clubs could continue in operation until the Park Service had the budget to replace them with a public beach, which, given other priorities and the proximity of the clubs to the huge public beach at Riis Park, could be many years in the future. All the other local controversies also turned out to be something that could be worked out, once the Park Service understood what the issues were.

I continued advising the Gateway project through all the planning stages and also the preparation of the necessary environmental impact statements, including spending time at working sessions in the main offices of the Park Service's planning staff at their Denver Service Center in Lakewood, Colorado.

The Sandy Hook peninsula in New Jersey, which forms part of the enclosure of the outer New York harbor, is part of Gateway. The plan called for a series of beach pavilions along the shore, as well as the restoration of the historic buildings of the former Fort

Hancock at the northern end of the peninsula. The Park Service prepared a detailed environmental impact statement, which mapped all the natural resources and included extensive descriptions of all the buildings. At almost the last moment, as the environmental impact statement was nearing completion, a representative of the U.S. Army confessed at one of our inter-governmental working sessions in Lakewood that when the army turned over Fort Hancock to the Park Service, it still had unexploded ordinance buried in the land from its days as a proving ground during World War I. A useful reminder about environmental impact statements: it is possible to look at every visible detail and still miss the most important issue, which required some revisions to the timing of the plan so that the ordinance could be located and removed.

Gateway has never been funded at a level that would permit the full development of the plan. As I write this, one of the Rockaway beach clubs is still there.

Planning and Design Workshops: Presentations to the community, like we made in the Bronx, do not give the community a real voice in what is being presented, only whether they like it or not. One answer to that problem is to start the planning process with a workshop. The workshop is publicly announced and is open to everyone, although the people who have the time and inclination to attend are not always representative of the whole community. The planners and designers who are leading the workshop begin by asking people to identify the big issues faced by the community, which are written down in some way that is visible to everyone. When people in the room are satisfied that everything necessary has been put forward, there is a short pause while the organizers of the workshop set up separate tables and chairs for each of the major issues identified, along with a means of recording discussions. The attendees choose which table they want to sit at, and each group discusses what should be done about the issue at that table. People are encouraged to have their say and then move to other tables if they wish to. Each table designates a reporter to communicate the conclusions from their discussion to the whole workshop. The whole concluding discussion is recorded and transcribed by the organizers and can then be sent to the participants and to others in the community. The planners and designers then are on notice what issues the participants feel should be addressed when the first iteration of the plan is presented at the next community meeting.

This process is far from definitive. People change their minds. The people who attended the workshop are not necessarily going to be the same people who come to the next presentation. But it is a way of building trust and communication (1.5).

Charrettes: At L'Ecole des Beaux Arts in Paris, generations of architects, including some Americans, were educated in a system where the designs they had made in their studios were collected at a deadline

1.5 A community workshop where each table is discussing a specific issue. People are free to move from table to table. At the end of the workshop, a spokesperson for each table reports its findings to the whole group.

and taken away to be judged and graded. The drawings that students had prepared, mounted on cardboard, were collected by functionaries and placed on a little cart, a charrette. According to legend, sometimes students would run besides the cart as it left the studio putting finishing touches on their presentations. The process of being faced with an imminent deadline was known to the students as being *en charrette*.

Among architects, working long hours to meet a deadline has become known as a charrette.

Andres Duany and Elizabeth Plater-Zyberk use charrettes in their urban design practice to improve communication with communities. They take their entire design process to a location within the community where they are working and make everything they do open to the public. People can come and go as they wish, observe, and even sit down and participate. The charrette typically goes on for four or five days, including a weekend at the end. There is a public progress report at the close of every day and a well-publicized public discussion of the completed presentation.

Of course, each charrette requires extensive preparation, and another six weeks or so are needed back at the office to prepare a final report. Getting the concentrated attention of designers and their consultants is efficient: they are likely to spend as many hours working on site as they would in a much longer process taking place in an office. I will describe the charrette for the Wildwood, Missouri Town Center in Chapter 7.

Bill Lennertz, an alumnus of the Duany/Plater-Zyberk office, has been a powerful advocate for using charrettes as the basic way of working with communities. He is now the president of the National Charrette Institute, based at Michigan State University, which has built up a long record of managing Charrettes on planning and design issues.

The Urban Land Institute's Panel Advisory Services, with groups of experts serving as volunteers, are also charrettes, although the public involvement is mostly meetings with key political and business leaders.

Working Committees: A working committee of local citizens can be appointed to respond to proposals by consultants, usually on issues where technical or political expertise from the committee members can be useful to the final result. These committee meetings can be open to the public, but the committee itself has the same member- ship each time it meets, solving one of the problems with a series of public presentations. The working committee for the village of Irvington, New York, is described in Chapter 2. In Omaha, we used both a working committee and a series of public presentations, as will be described in Chapter 9, with the working committee representing the city's decision makers reviewing the details of the presentations before they were made to the public.

A Typical Community Design Plan: Many cities, including Norfolk, Virginia, now adopt plans for each community as an agreed-upon guide to future development. I was the consultant in charge of the Greater Wards Corner Area Comprehensive Plan, prepared for Norfolk from 2002 to 2004.

We looked at the Wards Corner neighborhood, centered around an intersection located up a main street leading north from downtown, and near a highway interchange, as a potential uptown business and residential center. Our process required many meetings to explain our ideas to the community to get their agreement, or to find an accept- able alternative. The principles worked out at an initial workshop:

- Use city powers and new investment to eliminate blighting influ- ence of high-crime areas and encourage maintenance through comprehensive code enforcement
- Create a vibrant new mix of quality retail, entertainment, and local services responding to the needs and preferences of local resi- dents as well as the regional trading area
- Encourage a new, more urban pattern of development in Wards Corner, one with a lively mix of uses, a pedestrian orientation, and a renewed sense of place
- Encourage diversification of the housing stock, with quality higher density housing interspersed with retail to generate an active pedestrian environment, and enhance the scenic character and more efficient vehicular and pedestrian travel patterns along Little Creek Road and other highway corridors
- Improve amenities to help re-establish Wards Corner neighbor- hoods as among the most desirable in all of Norfolk for families of various economic means

1.6 A visualization of possible future development for the Wards Corner district in Norfolk, Virginia. Norfolk prepares plans to set city development policies for all the city's neighborhoods. These plans can be well in advance of actual development, as here, but the community and the city share a vision of what could be a desirable future.

An important part of each presentation was showing how the agreed principles could be translated into urban design concepts. One example: two strip shopping centers at the central Wards Corner intersection could be transformed into a place where apartment houses, built around courtyards, could have shops on their ground floors, and the current surface parking, which took up much of the land, would be decanted into parking garages. It is important in making such proposals that they are based on realistic projections of both market demand and financial feasibility. The economic consultants working with us on the plan thought such a proposal could work. We showed architecture derived from successful projects in other communities and demonstrated how it could fit into the site and create valuable public spaces as well (1.6). We also prepared comparable plans and perspectives for other, less dense parts of the neighborhood.

At the final meeting, after our presentation and discussion, Mayor Paul Fraim asked if there was anyone in the room who did not agree with the plan. One person raised his hand. "You're outvoted," said the mayor. The plan was adopted by the Norfolk City Council in November of 2004 and reaffirmed by the Council in 2009.

The Wards Corner area has since been identified as an important alternate location for intense development, as rising sea levels put the future of some other parts of Norfolk into question.

Wards Corner Now, a consortium of local organizations, has the plan prominently displayed on its website. But the strip shopping centers are still there. The community continues to be in favor of our proposals, but the owners of the two shopping centers are satisfied with their current returns and have not yet seen a reason to pursue more intensive development or to put their properties up for sale. But change is likely, particularly given what is happening to retailing because of e-commerce. And a clear vision of alternative possibilities remains available.[5]

Implementation strategies

Involving a community in design and planning has to begin with agreement about what the existing conditions are and what is needed to improve them. Then, the designer must explain the reasoning behind design proposals. Designers sometimes think that a design can be persuasive by itself, but many people can't look at design drawings and visualize how they apply to a particular situation, and a community has to understand why a particular design is a good choice for them.

A workshop with community members can be a good way to reach agreement on existing conditions. Then, a sequence of public presentations is always essential, beginning with showing potential alternatives, then about making choices among the alternatives, and finally agreement on specific designs and plans. This process takes time. It should not end until most of the people participating have become convinced that what they are seeing is the best design and planning solution for the current situation. There will always be some people who don't agree, but they should not be a large number.

A charrette can be a good way to telescope the decision-making process about a design, but its success will depend on how representative the community participants turn out to be. The design and planning consultants have an obligation to present alternatives which are feasible economically and politically.

It is no use reaching a consensus around ideas that cannot be implemented. At Twin Parks, we began with a definite allocation of housing resources from the city, which then stood behind the approved plan and worked out its implementation with the State's UDC.

However, when the Model Cities Program in New York City followed a comparable planning process to Twin Parks, much of the federal money that was expected to go to Model Cities, and was counted on for implementation, went instead to the Vietnam War. The result was that the community was brought to agreement on what should happen and then comparatively little actually happened. This kind of disillusioning experience can be worse than not doing a plan at all.

In the community-based Omaha by Design project described in Chapter 9, we were careful to have agreement from the Working Review Committee representing a wide spectrum of community leaders, investors, and city officials before we took any proposals to the public. Our final reports were approved, translated into regulations where appropriate, and continue to be implemented.

2

PROTECTING THE ENVIRONMENT

The natural environment is itself like a design, as it is created by the resolution of complicated, inter-related forces to produce a stable set of conditions. Often preserving or reinforcing the natural landscape can be the best urban and regional design strategy, but when zoning and subdivision laws were first enacted across the United States in the early years of the last century, they were blind to the natural environment. Zoning considers land a commodity assigned to different uses based on projections of future demand, without relating the different uses to the characteristics of the landscape. Development regulations and the standards for roads and highways were all set with the expectation that land can be engineered to take whatever shape is wanted. This assumption may have been acceptable when constructed development was only a small part of nature but has worked less and less well as increasingly large areas have become completely urbanized. There is often a critical mismatch between what is permitted and the carrying capacity of the land as a living ecosystem.

Ian McHarg brought attention to this problem in his pathbreaking 1969 book, *Design with Nature*,[1] making it emphatically clear that designers had to work within natural forces, and not against them, to avoid flooding, erosion, sinking water tables, and many other undesirable consequences. Unfortunately, relying on engineering to make development conform to regulations and rigid administrative standards still prevails almost everywhere, despite growing awareness that entire natural ecosystems are being destabilized as more and more urbanization expands across the landscape. Maintaining the sustainability of the natural environment has become a central urban design objective, but implementing it continues to be a difficult struggle against established laws and practices.

Preservation using park plans and planned development

One of the first projects we were asked to look at when we joined the New York City Planning Department in 1967 was the potential development of a large piece of still-rural land on Staten Island,

DOI: 10.4324/9781003384106-3

then the least developed of New York City's five boroughs. The publication of Ian McHarg's book was still two years in the future, but we already understood that the natural environment, like a community, was the pre-existing context and we should work with it, not against it.

A ridge ran across the site near the southern end; the land then sloped downward to the northwest. A stream meandered through part of the property, forming a shallow pond near the center of the site (2.1). We found out that the city had already prepared an official map for the whole area: a dense network of streets, designed as if all the land were flat and dry. Because streets in lower Manhattan had proved too small for the skyscraper district that ultimately grew up there, the engineers had designed these rural streets to not make the same mistake again. They were wide enough to support far denser development, which was highly unlikely to ever replace the attached or two-family houses zoned for the site (2.2). Implementing the official plan was in no one's

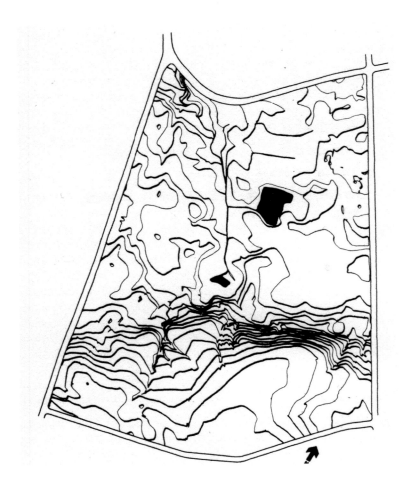

2.1 This large parcel of land in the New York City borough of Staten Island was still woods and meadowland in 1967. The map shows the land contours; there were no streets or buildings.

PROTECTING THE ENVIRONMENT

2.2 The City of New York had already prepared a street plan for the site: far too many streets, which were also much too wide, and no concern for the land contours or any other aspect of the natural environment.

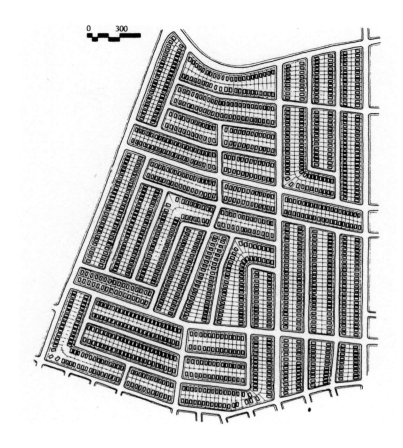

interest, including the developer, who would have to bulldoze and regrade the entire property and build more and bigger streets than were actually needed.

The ridge and stream formed a T-shaped space in the middle of the land. We thought it was an amenity that would make the whole development more desirable and should remain natural. To replace the pre-existing street plan, we proposed a series of looped streets into the site from the main thoroughfares around the perimeter of the property, leaving the steep slope of the ridge, the stream, and the pond intact (2.3). Norman Marcus, counsel to the Planning Commission, suggested that the way to make something like our plan possible would be to amend the zoning ordinance to create a planned unit development (PUD) option. PUDs have become a familiar way to expand urbanization into new areas, but they were then still a relatively new idea and had not been used in New York City. As the name suggests, a property can be planned as a unit, and the streets and lots shown in the plan can become the official street and subdivision map, if the overall development conforms to the zoning.

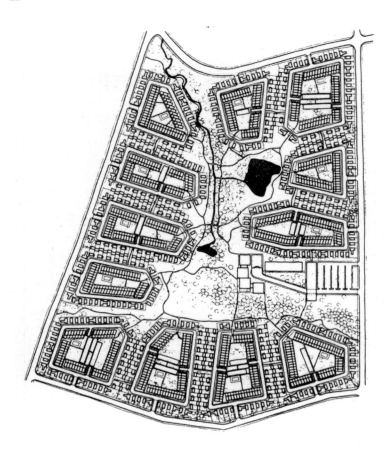

2.3 An alternative street and open space plan, prepared by the Urban Design Group of the New York City Planning Department, which the developers of the site accepted as a better option for them. Our plan included an elementary school which students could walk to via the open space, and a small shopping center.

We also looked at another option, simply amending the street map. Doing this would effectively take over the design of the site from the developer and would require a complicated negotiation. Instead, we recommended some architectural firms that we thought would manage the interests of both the developer and the city. The developer selected Norman Jaffe, who prepared a master plan for the whole site, which, while it differed from our drawings in some ways, realized our intentions. The city added PUD provisions to the zoning ordinance, and Jaffe's master plan was approved as the zoning and street plan for the site. Jaffe also designed the attached houses for the first four of the loop streets and the landscape around the stream and park. The master plan reserved land for a public elementary school and a neighborhood retail center, as we had suggested. Both have been built (2.4). We also prepared and published a book of standards for PUDs to show other New York City developers what would be required if they wished to use this option.[2]

An alternative method for preserving the natural environment was tried out by Edmund Bacon when he was the executive director of

PROTECTING THE ENVIRONMENT

2.4 New York City passed a Planned Unit Development amendment to the City's Zoning Resolution, a new technique at the time and never before used in New York. The site plan, approved as a PUD, was by architect Norman Jaffe. His plan was based on loop streets around a central open space, as we had suggested, and also followed our suggestions to include sites for an elementary school and a small shopping center, which have been built and appear at right in the photo. Jaffe also designed the attached houses with the gray roofs around the first four loop streets.

Philadelphia's Planning Commission. He used his city's street-design and park-management powers to lay out development for several thousand acres of what was then a still-rural part of north-east Philadelphia. Curvilinear streets were planned to form clusters of house lots along a continuous park system that preserves the land on both sides of the stream beds that run through the area. Implementation began in 1959. As land was acquired for development, each developer had to follow the street plan and dedicate to the city the land designated as park space. William H. Whyte writes approvingly of this North Philadelphia initiative in his book *The Last Landscape* but concludes that, "The result is not a showpiece. For so advanced a plan, what one sees on the ground is disappointingly ordinary."[3]

The advantage of Bacon's approach was that it dealt comprehensively with a larger area and saved significant parts of the natural environment from being bulldozed. The disadvantage was that the city of Philadelphia had little control over what was built along the streets. The local government has more say over what happens

2.5 While the street and open space plan approved in the original PUD continued to be used, later city administrations permitted a regression to very ordinary houses and apartments as development of the site was completed.

in PUDs, as the streets, open space, and proposed buildings are all part of the developer's submission for approval – but this control only applies to the individual property, not a larger region. The government also has to continue enforcing an approved PUD plan. What happened on Staten Island was that the first parts of the development, Village Greens, turned out well and still form a desirable community, but later city administrations permitted development of the site to revert toward the ordinary, although the open space is still preserved and children can walk through it to the school (2.5).

Neither PUD amendments or improved official street plans are enough to compensate for the way zoning and subdivision codes continue to ignore the natural environment. Even Ian McHarg was so intimidated by zoning rights that he illustrated in his book how woodland could be developed if the houses were just spaced far enough apart. But it would no longer be a woodland landscape if it had to accommodate the number of houses McHarg illustrated in his book, plus the streets and services needed to support them.

Correcting regulatory blindness toward the natural environment

Why should mature woodlands, steep hillsides, or wetlands, and especially land under water, have the same development entitlement as relatively flat, open, well-drained land? Lane Kendig said it should not, in his book, *Performance Zoning*, in which he suggested discounts for land that would be vulnerable to development when local governments compute what would otherwise be permitted in any zone. This calculation would then be followed by a PUD procedure to make sure that the vulnerable areas were not built upon. Kendig offered a way to make corrections to the existing regulations, site by site, without rewriting any of the basic rules. His book has never received the attention it deserved, possibly because the title does not describe the most important idea in the book. *Environmental Zoning* might have been a better name.[4]

Irvington Environmental Zoning: Kendig's book did come to the attention of the Board of Trustees of the Village of Irvington, New York. They were concerned that new development was flattening the landscape of their suburban village on the banks of the Hudson River, north of New York City. They asked planner Manuel S. Emanuel to help them rewrite part of their zoning code and asked me to make public presentations to the village illustrating the differences between conventional zoning and an environmentally based alternative. I recruited talented architect and urban designer Steven Peterson to work with me on this project. I have published some of our illustrations in my book, *The Fractured Metropolis*, along with a description of our Irvington planning process.[5]

The issue in Irvington was definitely not an example of an affluent community of single-family houses using the environment as an excuse to keep out affordable housing. Currently, about half the housing in the village consists of multi-family buildings: condominiums, cooperative apartments, and rental apartments, adding up to about 1,100 units. There are 1,180 single-family houses, many of them small, plus about 100 two- or three-family houses.[6]

What the community was concerned about was the way new subdivisions of expensive houses on large lots were leveling sites and taking away all the trees. The zoning in Irvington was based on minimum lot sizes that set the number of houses permitted per acre. The practice in Irvington, as in many other places, was to compute how many house lots could be developed on a particular property using what was called, literally, the billiard-table approach. The applicant could assume that the land was as flat and uniform as the surface of a billiard table and lay out the roads and house lots accordingly. This calculation determined the number of houses that could be fitted on the site and caused developers to make the land as close to a billiard table as they could.

To support changing the way Irvington approved development, the Mayor of the Village appointed a working committee to inform the consultants how the Village saw the problem, and respond to the proposals the consultants would make. The committee included several

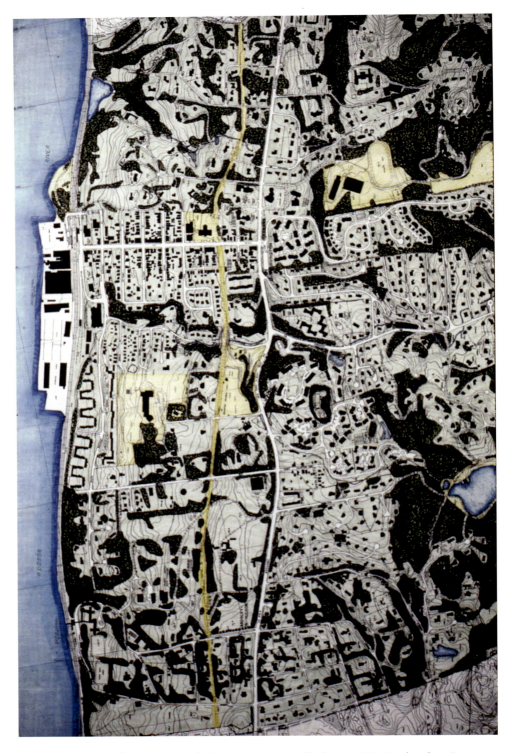

2.6 Figure 2.6 is a map of development in the western part of Irvington, New York, when Steven Peterson and I began our study.

PROTECTING THE ENVIRONMENT

2.7 New houses are shown in red which were likely to be developed if the zoning then in effect were to continue until this whole part of the Village was completely built out.

lawyers, as well as some experienced business executives. The meetings were open to the public, but the committee was in charge of the agenda.

For an early presentation to the committee, Steve and I drew a map showing the development of Irvington as it was at the time (2.6) and a visualization of a future Irvington where every available property had been developed according to the current zoning under its billiard-table interpretation. We did not exaggerate, simply showing what could happen if development continued to follow current practice (2.7). This strategy was effective in demonstrating the need for basing development on the carrying capacity of the land, and not on a notional billiard table. We then illustrated how that alternative could work with maps of smaller areas showing what new development would look like if environmental safeguards were included in the zoning.

The committee concluded that the Village should amend its zoning to discount the site area used in calculating development rights according to the land's vulnerability when destabilized by construction, as Lane Kendig had advocated. Article XV, Resource Protection, of the Village of Irvington's zoning, originally adopted in 1990 describes how an applicant for zoning approval must compute the amount of land that will be considered in determining what can be built in any zone.[7] First, the applicant must present an accurate survey of the land. The area of the property occupied by lakes, ponds, watercourses, Hudson River land, watershed land, wetlands, and floodplains must all be subtracted completely from the site area before calculating how much development will be permitted, as well as any land determined by the Planning Board to have unusual geological features. Three-quarters of any land that slopes at more than 25 degrees must also be subtracted, as well a half of all land with slopes between 15 and 25 degrees.

The resource protection zoning continues in force and Irvington has become an environmentally conscious community in other ways. Its adopted environmental action plan includes making the operations of the village more sustainable, working to improve stormwater management, and making the building code more encouraging to "green" building projects.[8]

Translating environmental designs into regulations

Requirements which relate development to the carrying capacity of the land are still exceptional, while the effects of climate change have made the disconnect between what is permitted by zoning and what can be managed within the natural landscape a more and more urgent problem. In our book, *Reinventing Development Regulations*, published by the Lincoln Institute of Land Policy in 2017, Brian Blaesser and I propose improvements for managing the relationship between construction and the natural environment based on my experience in Irvington and also drawing on our experience working together in Wildwood, and Omaha which will be described later in this book.[9]

Pair the Zoning Map with a GIS Map. Official zoning maps almost everywhere are still the same kind of two-dimensional street and property maps used since the 1920s. Local governments have depended upon detailed site maps submitted by developers when they apply for zoning or subdivision approval to make their decisions. Relying on the map for a specific site makes it unlikely that the approvals are made with a full understanding of how the new development will affect environmental conditions off site. Cities and towns now have much more information available to them from their Geographic Information Systems (GIS) than is included in traditional zoning maps. They can print out land contours, drainage systems, soil conditions, and aerial photos of existing buildings over the zoning map of streets and lots. While developers still need accurate environmental maps for their individual applications, the local government's GIS can give developers an overview of their site conditions at the very beginning of their decision-making, perhaps even before they buy, or option, a property.

Using GIS information and other scientific advice, communities can compile natural resource preservation plans that become the basis for keeping environmentally sensitive areas within their capacity to support development, somewhat like Edmund Bacon's plans for North Philadelphia back in the 1950s, but with a clearly articulated objective basis. Building on land that is subject to flooding or at risk from wildfire can also be restricted. In this way, the places unsuitable for buildings and streets are officially identified and zoned accordingly in advance, rather than waiting until there is a development submission for a fragment of the natural environment, as still happens under Irvington's zoning, despite its well-crafted resource protections.

To prevent developers from being tempted to clear sites of vegetation and regrade the landscape before coming in for approvals, Brian and I recommend that every community have a grading ordinance which requires a permit before any land can be disturbed, and that this permit should only be issued to implement an approved plan. A tree preservation ordinance is also needed to prevent large-scale removal of woodlands without a permit.

Remove the Same-Sized Lot Requirement: When planners decide that an area should have a specific development density – as an example, let us say a residential zone permitting no more than four houses per acre – the way this is accomplished in the regulations is by setting a *minimum lot size*. In this example, there could be four permitted lots for each acre, each no smaller than 10,000 square feet. An acre comprises 43,560 square feet, leaving some space available for access streets. Of course, a developer can have fewer, larger lots, but, to keep below the zoned density, every lot in the zone must be at least 10,000 square feet, with no more than four to the acre.

It is the minimum lot size requirement which produces the "cookie-cutter" communities where every house and lot is the same size, sometimes extending over developments for hundreds, and even thousands, of suburban houses.

PUDs permit a variation in lot sizes if the original density is maintained, as does another zoning device, traditional neighborhood development, written to make New Urbanist designs possible, as they seek to bring development back to a time before rigorous zoning separations. Both require a special procedure which is as complicated, and uncertain, as changing the zoning. There has to be a public planning hearing, followed by adoption of the alternative plan by the local legislative body, also after a public hearing.

The legal reasoning behind just eliminating the minimum lot size is the same as for a PUD or traditional neighborhood development: the underlying zoned density is not changed, and, if the zoning is for single-family houses, that does not change either. However, the houses could all be attached row-houses on 2,000 square foot lots, as long as there are no more than four of them per acre. In that alternative, there will be a considerable amount of land left undeveloped, which is part of the reason for eliminating the minimum lot size. Removing rigid lot size requirements makes it much easier to lay out streets and buildings to leave environmentally sensitive land in a natural state. Removing the minimum lot size also makes it easier to design compact, walkable neighborhoods.

Because eliminating the minimum lot size is a way to implement environmental protection criteria without diminishing what a developer is entitled to build, it is best considered in the context of environmental protection overlay zones based on criteria revealed by GIS mapping.

Subdivision proposals for street plans and building lots are always subject to planning review to make sure that they conform to the regulations. Proposals where there is no minimum lot size would still be subject to the same review procedure as any other subdivision.

Remove Numerical Grading Standards from the Subdivision Ordinance: One of the major reasons why developers "prepare a site for development" by bulldozing the hills into the valleys is the maximum street grade requirement in subdivision ordinances. This is set as a matter of law regardless of the location of a property. For relatively level sites, a set maximum street grade of 7 percent will not present much of a problem, but, if the terrain is hilly, it may be difficult to achieve it, especially as the slope of the house lots also has to be considered (you don't want the street dumping water into your yard during a rainstorm), and there are also requirements that street grades come down to something like 4 percent at intersections plus visibility requirements for drivers on one street to be able to see into the intersecting street, which implies that they need to be close to the same level. For a developer, leveling the entire site so it meets the administrative requirements everywhere can be the simplest solution.

The alternative is to require that street grades be approved as safe during the subdivision review process, but not to set a fixed numerical standard. Laying out the streets is a design problem, and it is best left to the design of the specific property. If there is no minimum lot size and the developer can cluster development on the less steep parts of a property without going through a complicated public approval process, it can be much easier to lay out safe streets and lots. The numerical standards for sloping streets are based on assumptions about driving speed, often assumed to be 30 miles an hour, an assumption that also underlies the minimum widths for streets, and the street curvature at intersections as set down in the subdivision ordinance. Designing streets that are safe but also fit the carrying capacity of the land should be permitted using criteria rather than numerical standards for street grades, lane widths, and their turning radius, as long as the local government's engineers are prepared to approve them, which could include designing streets for a slower speed, which will be much safer for pedestrians.

Require Stormwater Retention Measures: Preventing the first inch of rain in a downpour from flowing immediately into streets and storm sewers can greatly reduce the risk of flooding. Simply requiring driveways to be paved with materials that allow rainwater to flow through the driveway into the ground can make a big difference and new paving technologies make this possible. Having the roof drains of each structure flow into a rain barrel or cistern is another simple and inexpensive requirement, which can also give people a source of water for plants and for washing cars and decks without using purified drinking water. Pervious paving and cisterns for roof water can both be required in the building code and would apply to all new properties and any major renovations.

Require Green Parking Lots: Parking lots, especially at the size considered necessary for shopping centers and office parks, can become a major source of flooding as rainwater runs off from the parking lot's paved surfaces and overloads local drainage ways. Changing the design to keep the first inch of stormwater on the property is feasible if the parking lot has paving pervious to water, at least for the car spaces, and possibly for the access lanes as well. However, leveling acres of land to meet the grading requirements for the parking lots can destabilize the drainage of the surrounding area. Safe gradients should be achieved by terracing parts of the parking lot so they are adjusted to the natural slope of the land, not by flattening a large area and holding back the uphill and downhill sides with massive retaining walls.

Another problem with parking lots is that their hot reflective surfaces raise the ambient temperature of the areas around them, creating what are called urban heat islands. During extreme heat, parking lots can actually become dangerous places for some people. A way of mitigating heat in parking lots is to shade them. Regulations can require trees to be planted between rows of cars. The usual way of specifying the number of trees is by spacing them to a specific standard, such as trees should be planted on 25-foot centers. The tree species can be left to the property owner, or permitted trees can be listed in the regulations. An important regulatory issue is the continued existence of the required trees, an enforcement matter for inspectors from the building department.

Zone for Solar and Wind Access: One of the original reasons why communities adopted zoning codes was to safeguard access to light and air. Developers of one property should not be able to block sunlight and breezes from other properties. Preserving access to light and air today includes protecting the functionality of solar panels and preventing obstruction of access to wind energy. As more and more people install solar panels, protecting their access to sunlight becomes an even more significant issue. Local governments can use GIS to estimate the effects of new buildings on the solar access of surrounding properties. Wind access is more complicated; it requires analysis of how prevailing winds vary during the whole year. In the future, the zones that permit tall buildings may be mapped to optimize access to wind energy and to minimize negative effects on other zones.

A more complete discussion of these regulatory concepts, and the legal reasoning behind them, can be found in the first three chapters of Brian Blaesser's and my book, *Reinventing Development Regulations*, which can be downloaded at no charge from the website of the Lincoln Institute of Land Policy.

Implementation strategies

Wooded and agricultural land is not an empty space waiting for development, but part of a living ecosystem whose continued existence is essential for sustaining life on our planet. This idea is easy to accept in principle, but it can be strongly resisted "as a practical matter." Environmental safeguards can be written into regulations, including listing the types of environmentally sensitive land which must have their area deducted from calculations about zoning entitlements.

The central urban design strategy in both the Arden Heights and Irvington examples was to show the existing conditions, what would happen if the current development trend continued to be followed and the better result that could be achieved instead. The same approach, at the scale or the region and the megaregion, will be discussed in Chapter 10.

To support an urban design strategy directed at preserving the critical aspects of the natural environment, it is necessary to understand what they are. For Arden Heights and Irvington, we relied on the U.S. Geologic Survey maps. Today, Lidar-based computer mapping has provided a much more accurate tool for representing natural contours, vegetation, and drainage systems. Local communities can prepare comprehensive environmental protection plans using this kind of information and the advice of experts.

The community's zoning code should then be revised in accordance with this comprehensive plan to identify places that are sensitive to environmental degradation and should therefore be protected, and to identify natural systems within already urbanized areas that should be restored as much as possible.

It becomes easier to safeguard natural resources if zoning and subdivision codes are amended to remove the minimum lot size requirement – while preserving the zoned density – and substituting criteria for safety for numerical standards for street grading, lane width, and the radius of street curvature at intersections. The layout of streets is a design problem and should be treated that way.

Preventing erosion during torrential downpours can be achieved by devices for holding stormwater runoff within individual properties such as permeable paving and cisterns for roof water. Large parking lots need additional measures to manage stormwater runoff, including terracing, permeable paving, and trees. Shade from trees can also reduce the urban heat island effects generated by large parking lots.

Finally, renewable energy for individual properties can be supported by regulations which preserve access to sunlight and prevailing winds, requirements which are an extension of the original reasons for requiring zoning regulations.

3
DESIGNING CITIES WITHOUT DESIGNING BUILDINGS

Zoning and subdivision regulations are powerful urban design tools, although their effect on design is too often a by-product of requirements written for other purposes. It is possible to use development regulations constructively to redesign whole districts of a city, although it is a very different process from designing a group of buildings for a large property that is all controlled by one owner.

When we started working as the New York City Planning Department's urban design group in 1967, the city had just begun using a new zoning law, the first complete revision since the original ordinance had been adopted in 1916. Over the intervening 50 years, much of the city had developed in accordance with the old regulations and the replacement was an abrupt change. It introduced the floor area ratio as the means of controlling the size of buildings, relating them to the size of the property rather than the previous method which controlled the size of a building by limiting its height in relationship to the width of the street. The new law also gave a floor area bonus in the highest density districts for leaving part of the property as an open plaza – without saying anything about where on a property that plaza should be located, what it should look like, or even how accessible it would be. The new law was also far more rigorous in separating different kinds of permitted activities in each zone. Like all development regulations, the law also had nothing to say about whatever development already existed on any site, other than using up part, or all, of the assigned quota of floor area.

Some of the ideas behind the new zoning came from concepts promoted by the Congrès internationaux d'architecture moderne (CIAM) beginning in the 1920s. The aim of the CIAM was to replace all existing cities with an entirely different form of development: towers or long, slab buildings surrounded by open space, with working, living, shopping, and recreation each consigned to separate areas. The technicians who prepared New York's zoning law were not designers. They were trying to stay up to date, without understanding how destructive their new formulas could be.

We were asked to review the designs for the proposed buildings that were coming in for the Planning Commission's approval under the new regulations. We saw immediately that many of these proposals

DOI: 10.4324/9781003384106-4

would be a huge step backward for the city: destroying existing buildings that under the new floor area regulations had become more valuable dead than alive, placing new outdoor spaces where they weren't needed, and obliterating vital mixes of activities which in many areas would no longer be permitted.

We learned that the designs coming to the Planning Commission were a response to the city's own requirements. If the owners of the development wanted to maximize their profits, there would often be only one possible design that would meet their objectives. The city was getting exactly what it asked for.

How could we change this powerful tool so the city would be asking for buildings it actually wanted and needed?

There was no possibility of repealing the new regulations which had just been approved after years of discussion and revision. Norman Marcus, the Planning Commission's counsel, suggested that, instead, we could draw a boundary around areas of particular concern and add more regulations to what was already in the zoning. And, while we could not take away the floor area incentive for building plazas, we could also add incentives to support other objectives within these special zoning districts.

In a special zoning district, the land belongs to many different owners, the design and construction of individual buildings will go forward in an unpredictable order, and some properties may not develop at all. It may take several economic cycles before a design can take shape, and even longer before it is complete. The design concept built into the district regulations must be flexible enough to deal with such contingencies, but clear enough not to become lost as administrations and market conditions change.

Our first special zoning district was designed to protect New York City's unique concentration of legitimate theaters, which were under immediate threat from the development permitted by the new regulations. Following Norman Marcus's advice, we devised incentives to add new theaters when a site in the midtown theater district was redeveloped, which the Planning Commission adopted as the Special Theater Zoning District. The zoning change was soon supplemented by historic district designation for the existing theaters by the City's Landmark Preservation Commission. The combination has been successful in keeping the theater district together as a national and international destination. Another special zoning district was enacted to preserve Fifth Avenue in midtown New York as a unique specialty retailing location.

Lincoln Square: A completely implemented special zoning district

We also discovered that a special zoning district could be a way for the city to implement a specific urban design concept for an area that was likely to change completely – a way to design cities without designing the individual buildings.[1] The first of these districts was the Lincoln Square Special Zoning District. It has now been completely built out and can be looked at as an example of setting up an urban design to be implemented over a long period without controlling the architecture of the individual buildings.

The construction of the Lincoln Center for the Performing Arts had been expected to create new development around it and proposals were already coming into the Planning Commission. A whole section of the city could be transformed, but there was no design concept for the private development which would relate it to the performing arts complex. The opera house, concert hall, and dance theater were designed around a classical axis of symmetry within the rectangles formed by Manhattan's east-west streets. The central plaza opened out to Broadway, a street which dated back to the 17th century and cuts a diagonal path across the usual Manhattan grid.

The immediate catalyst for our intervention was a proposed residential tower across Broadway right on the central axis of Lincoln Center. We built a cardboard model of the Lincoln Center area, including the proposed new building, and brought together the whole urban design group to figure out what to do. Looking at the model, we could see how important it was that the miscellaneous collection of existing buildings along Broadway were all built right out to the edge of the sidewalk, which was traditional and was also the most advantageous way to build under the old zoning. The diagonal of Broadway was a foil to the axial symmetry of Lincoln Center, which followed the rectangular Manhattan Street grid, not the Broadway diagonal.

We saw that preserving the diagonal street space of Broadway could be a way to create coherence when new buildings were constructed, but, under the new regulations, there were likely to be plazas along Broadway as they had been given an incentive under the new zoning. If plazas were constructed, they could turn a coherent streetscape into a hodge-podge of unrelated open spaces. We hit upon the idea of including a build-to line in the special district we were proposing. A required setback line was already a familiar zoning concept. A build-to requirement is the opposite: all buildings must come up to the line, in this case drawn at the property boundary along the Broadway frontage. When developers chose to include a plaza, it would have to be elsewhere on the site, not along Broadway. However, we also did not want tall buildings rising to their full height directly from the Broadway frontage. We limited the height of the portion of the building along the build-to line to 85 feet, a dimension for base buildings which was already in the new zoning. Above 85 feet, we introduced a setback line, to distinguish the tower portion of new buildings, which would likely all be at different heights, from the uniform height of their base building.

The new zoning regulations already included an incentive to build an arcade along a street frontage. We decided to require an arcade in the same location as the build-to line, adding more specific dimensions to define what would be an acceptable arcade in this special district. We wanted the shop frontages along the arcade to support the performing arts center, so we amended the group of permitted ground-floor uses to include bars and restaurants, and to exclude uses like banks, or street-level offices for real-estate or insurance agents.

During our design session, Lauren Otis, a senior urban designer, picked up the tower part of the model for the first proposed building and turned it an angle that would make it the reciprocal of the geometry of Broadway – making the building on the Lincoln Center axis the center of the design composition for the special district. I am not sure we would have had the ability to require this, but the developer liked the idea and carried it out.

Our design requirements did not do much to change the underlying development economics, so the special district was not controversial. It was passed by the Planning Commission and approved by the Board of Estimate, then the city's legislature for these kinds of actions. It remains in effect, although the city later made the arcade optional. The map of the original special zoning district is shown in 3.1 and the map in the current ordinance is shown in 3.2.

The entire zoning district has now been implemented and has created a coherent organization for a whole section of the city (3.3). The arcades which were built are mostly used as seating for sidewalk cafes, which we hadn't thought of, but is a good way to use them. 3.4 shows the Broadway frontage after the COVID-19 pandemic led to sidewalk cafes being partially enclosed as "streateries."

The build-to line was an important innovation, used in many subsequent special districts, and became a key part of the required development of Battery Park City, designed by Alexander Cooper and Stanton Eckstut, alumni of the urban design group. Because the Battery Park City Authority owned the land, the build-to, setback, and façade requirements already used in the Lincoln Square Special Zoning District could be taken farther than was possible with zoning alone, including requirements about building materials. Developers bought the guidelines when they acquired their individual properties from the Authority. When some protested later, the Authority told them that they could sell the land to another developer if they did not wish to follow the agreement themselves.

Design guidelines in a property transaction

Implementing design requirements through a property transaction can work even in places with far weaker real-estate markets than New York City, although not always at the same level of detail possible at Battery Park City. I was a consultant to the Urban Redevelopment Authority in Pittsburgh, beginning in the late 1970s when much of the downtown redevelopment still relied on the government

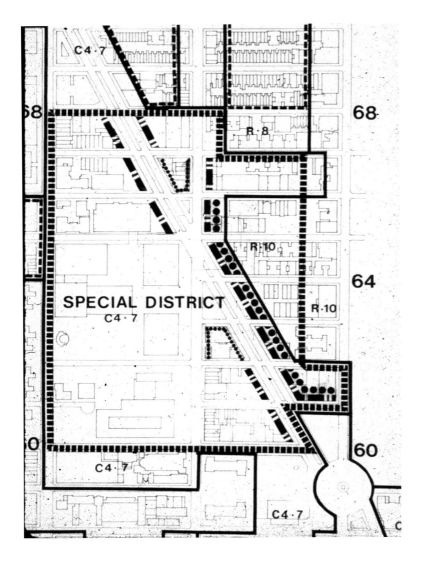

3.1 The original zoning map for the Lincoln Square Special District. The dash-dot-dash line denotes the build-to line, the consecutive large round dots define the location of the required arcade, and the lines of small round dots define blocks where change is subject to special rules because of the irregular shape of the sites. The requirement that the portion of the building at the build-to line must set back above 85 feet was in the text.

to assemble the sites. The Redevelopment Authority could write design guidelines that became part of the contract transferring the property to the new owner. One of my first assignments was drafting the design guidelines for the PPG Industries (Pittsburgh Plate Glass) headquarters. PPG had already conducted a search of possible locations for their new corporate headquarters in other cities, and then made a deal with the Urban Redevelopment Authority to obtain five and a half acres of downtown land, mostly small commercial buildings, just east of the office buildings in the Gateway Center, Pittsburgh's first cluster of post-World War II buildings. The Redevelopment Authority made a finding of blight, which allowed them to acquire the properties; and PPG financed their acquisition. Under redevelopment law, a blighted district could include viable

DESIGNING CITIES WITHOUT DESIGNING BUILDINGS

3.2 This is the current Lincoln Square Special District map in the New York City zoning resolution. Building at the property line is now described as the Street Wall and is required to be 85 feet high above street level before a setback. There are also additional Street Wall requirements: 125 feet on the Central Park West frontage and 125 feet on a small triangular parcel at one of two focal locations along Broadway, and 150 feet on the other. The arcade requirement has been eliminated.

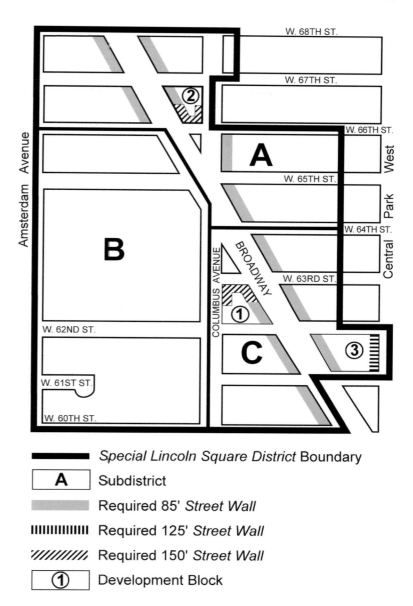

— Special Lincoln Square District Boundary
A — Subdistrict
— Required 85' Street Wall
|||||||||| — Required 125' Street Wall
///////// — Required 150' Street Wall
① — Development Block

individual buildings, and some of the acquisitions were controversial. The owner of a hardware store put up a huge sign on the front of his building: Blight Means Somebody Else Wants Your Building. The owners of these downtown commercial properties could afford to retain lawyers and obtain substantial financial settlements, which PPG Industries had to pay.

Since a typical office tower would not need much more than an acre of the five and a half acres acquired for PPG, I made sure that the guidelines included language requiring all the land to

3.3 This aerial view shows the different ways the 85-foot build to the front property line/Street Wall requirement has been followed by the architects and developers for the buildings along the east side of Broadway. Lincoln Center is in the upper left-hand corner of the picture.

be occupied by PPG buildings suitable for an urban setting. That meant no vacant plots used for parking until some vaguely identified phase 2, and no suburban-style lawns and plantings deployed to use up the rest of the land.

After a national search, PPG chose Philip Johnson and John Burgee as their architects. They had recently completed the design for the A. T. & T. Building (now 550 Madison Avenue) in New York, where

DESIGNING CITIES WITHOUT DESIGNING BUILDINGS 41

3.4 This photo shows how the consistent Street Wall looks at ground level. The arcades became the locations for sidewalk cafes. Since the COVID-19 pandemic, some of these cafes have been enclosed as "streateries." Without the zoning requirements, the spaces along the street would have been as varied as the towers above, shown in the previous view.

Johnson had gone back to something like the masonry façades used in office buildings before the much lighter glass curtain wall had supplanted them. He had made public statements that "the glass building is dead."

But now Johnson was designing the headquarters of a glass company and the glass building turned out to be alive after all. He proposed a crystalline reinterpretation of 19th-century gothic revival buildings and found ways to use the entire five and half acres, while following the guideline requirements for scale and land use. To use all the land, he persuaded PPG to build a new urban square, entirely their own, in front of the tower and surrounded by low buildings. He designed ground-floor retail frontages for the parts of the buildings facing the adjacent Market Square, another guideline requirement. The parking garage is on the opposite side of the square from the tower, so people would cross the open space on their way to the offices (there is also an underground connection). He also included an enclosed winter garden west of the tower (3.5 and 3.6).

For a long time, the tenants of the shops in the PPG frontages along Market Square did not want to use their Market Square entrances, as they also had entrances from inside the building. The stores were boutiques directed toward the employees. The store owners didn't want to monitor two doors and they didn't want the people hanging out in the Square coming into their shops. So they kept the doors locked. Not only that, the Market Square side of the stores was used for storage. As you walked by, you would see boxes piled up against the locked glass doors. The city went through a number of attempts to revitalize Market Square, but, until the traffic engineers permitted closing Forbes Avenue, which ran through the middle of the Square, nothing worked. Finally, something like 25 years later, Forbes Avenue was closed and the Square was redone to a simple, but effective, design and became the food and restaurant destination the city had always intended. Now, the PPG frontages have restaurant tenants, the doors open, and that side of their building complex participates in the life of Market Square.

The PPG headquarters met the public policy objectives. Should the city have asked for more? Rather than straining to spread the program across the whole site, could PPG have built a mixed-use project, perhaps with some residential buildings? We did have discussions about this possibility, including asking PPG to consider architects with experience in designing downtown commercial developments. PPG definitely wanted a completely corporate setting and the city did not think it had the leverage to require a development program that risked not being successful.

Design review

Every building must receive a permit from the local government's building department before construction can begin. But building departments are not expected to make discretionary decisions. They can review for compliance with specific metrics, like the distance of a setback from an adjacent structure, but questions about whether a proposed subdivision plan meets the legal requirements, or whether a new building complies with the constraints of a historic district,

DESIGNING CITIES WITHOUT DESIGNING BUILDINGS 43

3.5 An aerial view of downtown Pittsburgh from Google shows PPG Industries' office campus. Market Square in the foreground has been renovated by the city and has become a bar and restaurant destination. The simple but effective redesign of the Square is by Klavon Design Associates. The low buildings belonging to PPG in the upper right-hand quadrant of Market Square were always intended to be in scale with Market Square and now reinforce it by having restaurants on their ground floors. In the center of the picture, in front of the main office tower, is PPG's own square, called PPG Place, completely surrounded by the consistent glass facades devised by architects Philip Johnson and John Burgee.

3.6 PPG Place seen at street level from Third Avenue, enclosed by the glass facades designed by Johnson Burgee Architects. In good weather, you can pick up your lunch at one of the restaurants in the area and dine out under the umbrellas. The main entrance to the office tower is at left.

should be referred to agencies that are equipped to make these evaluations well before the contract documents are ready for review by the building department.

Site Plan Review by Planning Departments: Planning Agencies have the power to review and approve the site plans of residential subdivisions, planned unit developments, or traditional neighborhood developments to make sure that the design conforms to the provisions of the ordinance. Site plan review can also apply to other situations where the site plan is more complicated than an individual lot.

In Pittsburgh in the 1980s, as confidence in the viability of downtown increased, development took place without the city being asked to help with property assemblage. Pittsburgh's zoning code gave the City Planning Department site plan review authority over almost all development except small residential buildings. Robert Lurcott, the planning director, preferred the term Project Development Plan Review to emphasize that it was about three dimensions, not just what is visible in a plan. Paul Farmer, then the deputy planning director, was a strong advocate for using the city's site plan review powers to safeguard the public interest in new developments. As the planning department's consultant, I suggested that they issue design guidelines when developers notified the city that they intended to apply for zoning approval, so that everyone understood what the city's design priorities would be. I worked with planning staffers Fred Swiss and

Mark Bunnell preparing these guidelines. The case for the planning department's priorities was backed up by a more general Downtown Development Strategy, plus standards for street design, including the sidewalks which in Pittsburgh as in many other cities are the responsibility of the property owner. I also worked with Fred and Mark preparing these two documents.

Many of the planning and zoning policies incorporated in the guidelines were related to making the city more walkable. Loading and unloading should take place within each building behind closable doors. Trucks should not protrude from an open loading dock and block the sidewalk and part of the street. Bins full of garbage and rubbish should not be visible from the sidewalk. The location of entrances and exits for loading and parking should not cut into retail frontages. The vaults for electrical transformers serving a building should not take up an entire sidewalk. The sidewalks themselves should meet the city's street and sidewalk standards — no more inexpensive asphalt sidewalks that became sticky in hot weather. Sometimes, review caught a problem that had not been anticipated, as when I saw that the plans for a downtown hotel placed the exhaust fans from the hotel kitchens so they would blast onto the sidewalk right at eye level. I don't think the hotel architects, used to designing for suburban sites surrounded by parking, had given this decision any thought. They came up with an acceptable alternative.

Design Review in Historic Districts: Charleston, South Carolina has one of the first and most extensive historic district designations. Demolitions, repairs, and new construction within the Old and Historic District must first secure approval by the Board of Architectural Review, which gives the city substantial control. A developer cannot assemble properties, tear down the buildings, and then come in for a permit for new development. Developers with plans for a new building or a renovation within the historic district need to talk to the City of Charleston about their plans and work with the staff – and on important projects with the mayor – to prepare a proposal that would be acceptable to the Board of Architectural Review. When I was a consultant to the City of Charleston, I would be asked to make suggestions during these preliminaries.

I would sometimes attend a session of the Board when I had been involved in one of the projects before them. What is appropriate in a historic district? Charleston's Old and Historic District is unusual because it includes the entire central area of the city. More usually, a historic district is much smaller and has a specific design character established at a particular time in history. In Charleston, the Board had to decide what was appropriate for a new convention center hotel or a new office building, structures which were larger in scale than the buildings that established the historic character. I believe that the best approach to design review in such a complex situation would be to articulate the criteria for review before the architects prepared a design, as had been done in Pittsburgh, and the Board was definitely not in favor of doing this. Long after I was a consultant in Charleston, during Joe Riley's last term as mayor, he retained Andres Duany and Marina Khoury of Duany/Plater-Zyberk and Partners to prepare criteria for design review. By that time, the purview of the Board of Architectural Review had been expanded northward up the Charleston Peninsula and took in many areas where proposals were primarily for new construction.

Design Review Boards: The Architectural Review Board in Wildwood, Missouri – described in Chapter 7 – and the Urban Design Review Board for Omaha, Nebraska – described in Chapter 9 – are both intended to review any project referred to them by the planning department, as well as any structure being built by the city, or on city property. They are advisory to decisions made by the planning authorities, but their recommendations can have more weight than reviews conducted solely by designers on the planning staff. Members of a design review board can work informally with the development's design professionals to explore design alternatives. If there is a good working relationship and the suggestions make sense to the developer, there can be opportunities to go farther than what the authorities can require.

Criteria for design review or special zoning districts

When a design review board or a historic district commission reviews a proposed building, it can clarify the discussion if there are adopted criteria available for making judgments about the proposal. The criteria can take the form of an illustrated handbook of what is expected, as was compiled for the Wildwood town center described in Chapter 7. It is also possible to provide more explicit criteria, as was done for the Art Commission in Cleveland as described in Chapter 4, by mapping some familiar zoning requirements and using them to define what is expected.

There are three important categories of the public interest in the design of private properties that are visible from, and relate to, a community's streets and public spaces. The first is the building's placement in relation to the street and adjacent buildings, involving height limits, build-to lines, setback lines, as at Lincoln Square. The second is the land use at the street level and the third is the location and treatment of entrances for pedestrians, and also for garages and loading docks.

Setbacks: Setbacks from the lot lines are typical in zoning districts to provide light and air for neighboring properties. For small buildings, they create front, side, and rear yards. In larger buildings that are permitted to build to the front and side property lines, setbacks are frequently required above prescribed heights.

Height Limits: Height limits have a long history in development regulations and are widely used. A height limit in low-density residential zones is a typical zoning requirement. A frequently used number is 35 feet. That leaves enough room for three residential stories and a pitched roof. But 35 feet above what? Above grade is an answer, but what is grade on a sloping site? Above the lowest point on the property? Above the highest? Above the average? The usual answer is the average grade. Many zoning codes prevent the building owner from slipping an extra floor onto the site by also explicitly limiting the number of stories.

A height limit can be a review criterion and it can also be enacted as part of a zoning district to keep new development in scale with an officially designated historic district or with the existing built context. The limit can simply apply to the whole district or it can be used in combination with a setback requirement to limit the height of the lower portion of the building to a prescribed level but permit higher development within the setbacks. The Lincoln Square special district was an early use of build-to lines combined with height limits for the lower portions of the buildings with setbacks for the towers.

Build-to Lines: The build-to lines we used in Lincoln Square are the opposite of setbacks, requiring that the façade of a building must be placed at a line, in that case the front property line. Sometimes, to avoid unnecessarily rigid control over a building design, the build-to requirement can be for a percentage of the façade, usually at least 70 percent. Combined setback and build-to lines can be used in residential development to create a uniform depth for front yards. On a commercial street, a build-to line can be used to create or preserve continuity for retail frontages. In a historic district, or for respecting the existing built context, the build-to line can be placed at the front property line, or at a location which is an average for the historic development.

Transparency Requirements: Where blank walls may be part of a possible development, a review criterion can be a percentage of the wall area that must be entrances or windows. This requirement can be particularly important for ground floors in retail districts. Again, transparency can be written into a zoning district as percentages of wall area, but achieving it requires design review and should not be left to the building department.

Location and Masking of Services: No one wants to walk down a busy sidewalk and be confronted by an open service dock filled with dumpsters, or by a truck backed into the dock and blocking the sidewalk. Language in the zoning text can require that all service activities take place within the building line and be shielded from public view. The location of parking and service entrances and exits, often referred to as curb cuts, can also be regulated. In downtown areas, Andres Duany suggests distinguishing between A streets and B streets. Shopping frontages might define an A street, with services and parking access around the corner on a B side street.

In lower-density residential districts, the number of curb cuts can be limited to one for each property, to keep sidewalks walkable.

Conformity to Historic Styles: What are called historic architectural styles can be required to make new development conform to an existing historic district. Santa Barbara, California and Nantucket, Massachusetts are examples of places where there are design handbooks to show what is expected of new development. Appropriateness is definitely an issue that should be given to a review commission to decide, and not the building department.[2]

Streetscape designs

A local government has the power to design streets, and it should use it, and not just let streets be the default result of separate engineering considerations. A streetscape handbook can describe what fixtures and materials to select and also how everything should be placed within the right of way. Streetscape elements include street, sidewalk, and crosswalk paving, curb materials, drainage catch basins, and the dimensions for each, and the placement of what is called street furniture: streetlights, pedestrian crosswalk lights, sidewalk lighting fixtures, traffic information signs, parking information signs, fire and police alarms, newspaper and other vending machines, as well as trash and recycling receptacles. People don't generally pay much attention to the design of all the things they see on street; they become a kind of noise. But a street where all these elements have been organized as part of a design plan can be a very different experience.

I prepared a streetscape handbook for Norfolk, Virginia, working with landscape architect, James Urban. The most unusual part of the handbook is how it dealt with street trees. Jim is an expert on keeping trees alive in urban settings. Urban trees are often confined to small planting beds, called tree pits, but the roots are roughly as extensive as the foliage of the tree although in a different configuration. Jim's explanation: "Think of a wine glass on a dinner plate." If a tree tries to grow past the limits of its root system, it will die, the reason behind the tradition of pollarding (severely cutting back) street trees, frequently seen in Europe. Jim's prescriptions include planting trees along streets in continuous trenches, rather than confining them to individual tree pits. Additionally, bricks or other kinds of sidewalk pavers set in sand rather than concrete can let water percolate through to tree roots. Another problem that needs to be solved is keeping a tree watered until it is well-established, which, unless individual building owners will take care of it, requires some kind of drip irrigation system as part of the original planting (3.7).

Today, in addition to the usual streetscape components, local governments have to consider including bicycle lanes, using the street space as part of a green infrastructure system for managing stormwater (3.8), and possibly revising street and sidewalk configurations and dimensions as driverless vehicles start to become part of the traffic pattern.

DESIGNING CITIES WITHOUT DESIGNING BUILDINGS

49

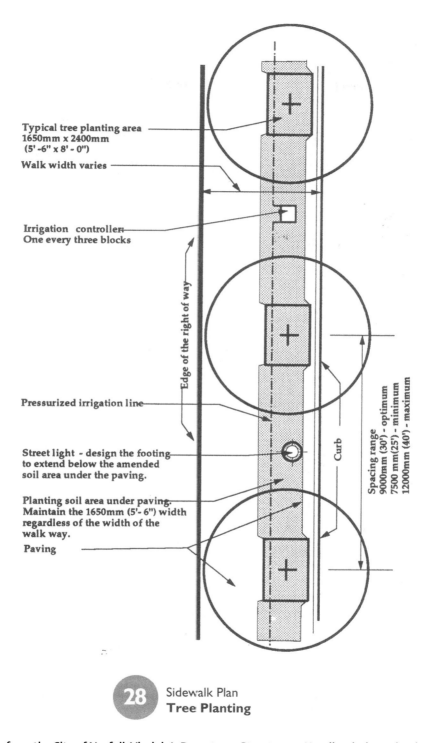

3.7 A page from the City of Norfolk Virginia's Downtown Streetscape Handbook shows landscape architect James Urban's prescriptions for keeping street trees alive by planting them in continuous trenches and supporting them with an irrigation system until the trees become established.

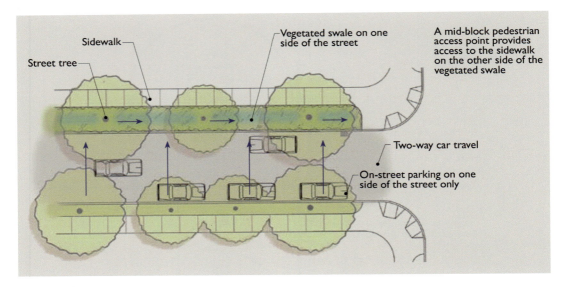

3.8 As heavy downpours become both more frequent and more intense because of a changing climate, street rights of way will be needed to help manage stormwater. The illustration shows trees planted in a vegetated swale, sometimes called a rain garden, along one side of a suburban street. The street is designed so that stormwater will drain into the swale and will be held there while the storm passes through, with the water eventually filtering down into the ground. Preventing the first inch of rain from running off immediately into drains and streams diminishes flood risks. Irrigation from rainwater helps support the trees. Street crossing are limited in this design to the corners and the mid-blocks. The illustration is from a stormwater management handbook published by the U.S. Environmental Protection Administration. The handbook was prepared by Nevue Ngan Associates, Eisen|Letunic, Van Meter, Williams Pollack LLP, and ICF International.

In addition to my work in Norfolk, I helped put together the Pittsburgh City Planning Department's streetscape standards and advised the New York City Transportation Administration about streetscape designs. In my experience, the biggest problem with streetscape standards is getting people to follow them. An initial installation can follow the handbook by incorporating its designs in construction drawings either for a local government or for a private investor who is responsible for constructing streets and sidewalks in a subdivision, or sidewalks in an urban setting. Construction documents can be reviewed for compliance before construction begins. But maintenance is done by crews working in the field and they are not usually going to refer to a handbook. The provisions in the handbook have to become part of the customary working process, both for ordering materials and fixtures and for installing them.

Implementation strategies

Well-established zoning mechanisms like setbacks, height limits, and build-to lines can be used creatively to guide development in special zoning districts, and in overlay zones which reinforce historic district designations. They can also become part of property agreements when a government agency or a private master developer sells a parcel of land to a developer or an individual owner. These private agreements can be more detailed than requirements administered through zoning. Any development on such a property must follow the guidelines which the buyer has agreed to as part of the purchase.

Special zoning districts should require that the planning authorities provide a certificate of compliance before a building permit is granted. In a historic district, the agency that administers the historic district must approve the proposed development. Building guidelines for land purchased through an agreement with a public agency should require a letter of approval before a building permit is issued. If guidelines are part of a private transaction, as in many New Urbanist communities, it is up to the master developer to enforce the agreement.

Planned unit developments and traditional neighborhood developments should recuire approval by the planning authority and the local legislature. A subdivision plan which complies with the zoning still should require review and approval by the planning authority.

As a general principle, implementing urban design concepts will be most effective if requirements are clearly articulated in a published book of standards and examples, and are then maintained consistently, becoming an understood and accepted part of the development context.

A well-designed city has streetscape design standards which are used for all new installations and maintained consistently. The need to make room for green infrastructure, accommodate more bicycles and other personal forms of transport like scooters, and adjust to the introduction of driverless cars and delivery vehicles will mean that achieving a coherent design for the streetscape is going to become both more difficult and more important.

4
ENHANCING PUBLIC OPEN SPACES

Public open spaces can be gathering places for major events and can also be refuges for people needing a break from the frantic pace of urban life. They can be a focus of civic pride and they can create value for the surrounding real-estate. But the design of the space should create a place where people want to be, and effective public spaces can cost public money, which is also needed for many other competing government projects. Often creating a desirable public space requires a strategy that links the design and construction of the space to other public or private objectives.

Nashville Public Square

Public Square in Nashville was part of the original street system of the city, laid out by Thomas Molloy in 1784, but for most of its history Public Square was the location for various municipal buildings, including Nashville's city hall, jail, and market; it was not primarily a public open space. The current Nashville Metro Government City Hall and the Davidson County Courthouse are combined in one building, completed in 1937, at the center of what was then Public Square, taking up most of the land. It is a symmetrical, neo-classical building, with *art moderne* details, by the partnership of Frederick Hirons and Emmons Woolwine. By the 1970s, a new space in front of this building had been created by clearing an entire block of late 19th- and early 20th-century structures, many of which would have been eligible for historic district designation today. The resulting space was called Public Square, but it was used as the parking lot for workers in the city hall and courthouse. In 2002, the administration of Mayor Bill Purcell of the Nashville-Davidson County metro government decided to make this parking lot into a real public square.

Wallace Roberts and Todd (WRT), which had recently completed a master plan for the Metro Nashville Park system, was asked to prepare a small feasibility study showing how to turn the parking lot into a public square. I had recently joined WRT as a consulting principal, and this was the first project they asked me to work on. I wrote a short report, illustrated by sketches, working with Ignacio Bunster, the partner in charge of landscape architecture in the Philadelphia office. We described several different design alternatives as a way to get Metro

DOI: 10.4324/9781003384106-5

thinking about what kind of a space they would prefer. I presented these designs in Nashville to a committee chaired by David Manning, the metro government's finance director.

The committee liked the designs, but they thought that decisions about them would be a long way in the future, because, as I learned at this meeting, Metro was very concerned to maintain the parking, and to add more of it. They intended to build an underground parking garage first and only then go on to the design and construction of the public space on top. I explained to the committee why that approach would not work. If the engineering for the garage did not include a public park on top, the design for whatever park or plaza was added later would have to be supported by the garage structure they had just put in place. If a typical parking garage structure would support a landscaped plaza at all, which was far from certain, the structure of the garage, and especially the roof, would determine what could be done with the public space above it. I said that the park and garage should be designed together and – where there was a potential structural conflict – the design of the public space should take precedence if at all possible.

David Manning had not heard about this issue before either from the parks department or from the transportation department which was in charge of building the garage. He asked me to explain in more detail, which I did: describing how uniform loads like soil and paving, and the people walking on them, would have to be carried by beams to the supporting columns, and both would have to be designed to carry them. Point loads – like trees – would very likely require additional supporting structures or be located outside the garage structure. Manning then went around the table asking if everyone agreed with my concerns. They did.

Metro wrote a contract for WRT to design Public Square while working closely with Walker Parking Consultants as they designed the garage. The phases of design for the garage and for the park would be completed and approved at the same time. Ignacio would be the landscape architect for the park, but David Manning insisted that I continue to be involved.

The garage definitely influenced the design of the public space. There was a limit to how deep the excavation for the garage could go without water seeping in from the Cumberland River a short distance away. To accommodate the thousand cars Metro wanted, the roof structure of the garage ended up being noticeably higher than the adjacent streets. The garage also required ventilation shafts and places where exit stairs could come up to the surface.

The central elements of the completed design are a large oval lawn and a terrace in front of the courthouse building. They occupy much of the garage roof (4.1). They are good places for holding events and are in keeping with the symmetrical architecture of the courthouse

4.1 The completed Nashville Public Square seen from above. The design for the terrace and oval lawn in front of the city hall/courthouse responds to its architecture and puts a relatively small load on the structure of the garage below. Around the periphery of the Square, beyond the garage structure, there is room for trees to frame the space. The reflecting pools and the main central entrance are lined with granite pylons displaying elements of Nashville's history. The park design is by WRT with Hawkins Partners and Tuck-Hinton.

building, but they also put much less weight on the garage structure than a more heavily landscaped park space, even when a lot of people come to a concert in front of the courthouse. Substantial groups of trees are planted around the perimeter of the Square, away from the garage structure. The perimeter of the square has been designed with broad flights of steps to manage the transition between street levels and the park (4.2).

Our design team included two Nashville architectural firms, Hawkins Partners and Tuck-Hinton. They worked with us to make the south side of the park, where there was more freedom from the garage structure, into an outdoor museum of Nashville history. Two reflecting pools run the length of the southern end of square, separated by a walkway leading into the Square from the southern entrance. Granite pylons holding illustrations of historical events line the south sides of the reflecting pools and both sides of the walkway. There is also an observation platform on the center axis of the east side of the oval.

There is an entrance and exit for the parking garage off Robinson Boulevard next to the north side of the courthouse, and a second entrance and exit for the lower levels of the garage off Gay Street, below the park near the banks of the Cumberland River. Inside Public Square, there is little to remind you that it is built over parking.

I made presentations about our design for Public Square to the Nashville Civic Design Center, which Mayor Bill Purcell encouraged the city staff and consultants to use as a sounding board for policies and projects. The tone set by these meetings was somewhat accusatory: the people around the table at the Civic Design Center seemed convinced that we were up to no good. However, they did not oppose the design. In fact, the WRT design for the Square fit right into the Civic Design Center's *Plan of Nashville* document published some years later, which followed the principles of traditional urban design, with axes already implicit in the downtown street map strongly emphasized and blocks re-planned as mid-rise courtyard buildings on the pattern of central Paris in the 19th century. The Civic Design Center included a drawing of the WRT design for Public Square in their plan, but without mentioning WRT. A careful reader can find the design credited, in very small letters, to Hawkins Partners, one of our subconsultants, whose principals had been among the founders of the Civic Design Center.

The completed Square has become accepted as one of Nashville's landmarks. It looks as if it was part of the original design for the city hall and courthouse and had been there all along.

The Milwaukee RiverWalk

Robert Beckley, a professor of architecture at the University of Wisconsin, Milwaukee, had a vision for downtown Milwaukee: it should have a pedestrian concourse on both sides of the Milwaukee River, in some ways like the celebrated Riverwalk in San Antonio. Milwaukee architect Alfred Clas had suggested something similar many years before, but the Clas proposal had been to narrow the bed of the river and build streets and sidewalks on both sides. Beckley saw that pedestrian connections could be accomplished without a major public works project using walkways linking each property to its neighbors, sometimes by cantilevering the walkway out over the river. He made the design studio he was teaching in the spring semester of 1981 a way to help people in Milwaukee visualize this idea and invited me to give urban design advice as an Eschweiler Visiting Professor.

Bob set up the studio like a professional consulting project, with the students developing an overall concept plan, and then having each student prepare a detailed design for a place within the plan. Having a whole design studio work on a project is a big-advance in people-power over the staffing of most consulting studies. However, the students are not being paid; on the contrary, they are paying tuition for an experience that will help them to develop as designers.

56　　　　　　　　　　　　　　　　　　　　　　　ENHANCING PUBLIC OPEN SPACES

4.2　The underground garage raised the Nashville park above the surrounding streets. The transitions are carefully managed by broad flights of shallow stairs.

Students have the final say on their designs; their teachers can't tell them what to do the way they might direct an employee. On my periodic visits to the studio, I worked with the students on the overall map describing what could happen, and then with individual students to show them what aspects of architecture were important for an urban design proposal. I told them they were not expected to show projects that were economically feasible, but they ought to be able to tell a plausible story about how their project could be implemented. I thought the students did a good job. The map they produced together, the primary urban design document, clearly showed how pedestrian walkways along the river would open up a second frontage for both existing and new buildings, which would have real economic benefits for the building owners as well as for the city. Most of the buildings the students designed illustrated how these two frontages would work and made a good case for a riverwalk.

Bob set up the students' final presentation like the conclusion of a consulting study. Some city officials, community leaders, and press were invited; and there was even a press kit summarizing the plan, complete with photos of the projects. There was coverage in the Milwaukee Sentinel the next day, although the headline was Condo-Bridge Plan Revealed. The reporter had picked up on one of the more striking, but less plausible, student projects where a bridge across the Milwaukee River was shown to have been redesigned to accommodate apartments.

CH2Mhill, a major engineering firm,[1] had been retained in 1977 to figure out how to clean up the Milwaukee River, and they were nearing the completion of their work, which included opening the gates of a dam upstream that had restricted the flow of the river. They became aware of the riverwalk concept and decided it could be a good way to demonstrate the difference a clean river would make for the city. They found the funding to support Bob Beckley and his architectural partner Sherrill Myers in preparing an urban design plan for the Milwaukee River downtown. The plan included walkways on both sides of the river, restaurants and apartments facing the water, and public access at the ends of streets where they ended at the river's edge.

The Greater Milwaukee Committee, the business leadership group, adopted the urban design plan as a project of the year. Mayor Henry Maier was shown the drawings and decided the riverwalk plan should be incorporated in the city's master plan. The city's department of development took the plan to the next level of detail with its Riverlink project which included river taxis and programmed events.

In 1988, the next mayor, John Norquist, announced a Riverwalk Initiative that became the Milwaukee Riverfront District and included a funding mechanism where the city would pay for part of the construction of riverwalk segments on private property: 70 percent of walkway construction costs up to $2,000 per linear foot and 50 percent of the dock wall costs up to $800 per linear foot.[2] In the early 1990s, the developer of a new building on the river designed the project to open up the river frontage and build a walkway. Other building owners, seeing the benefits of a second frontage along the river, partly subsidized by the city, began to remodel their properties. By 1998, the first eight blocks of what was now named the RiverWalk were substantially complete.

Today, the Milwaukee RiverWalk is three miles long, made up of three continuous segments. Sometimes, it is just a narrow walkway, but often it opens out to terraces and restaurants (4.3). In many places where streets meet the riverfront, there are special landscaped

4.3 A pleasant evening along the Milwaukee RiverWalk. The construction of the walkways creates a valuable commercial frontage, financed by the individual building owners with help from a construction subsidy by the City.

4.4 The Milwaukee RiverWalk is closely tied to the downtown sidewalk system, unlike the famous River Walk in San Antonio which is a story below street level. Sometimes, Milwaukee's walkway is only a narrow connection, but it often widens out into terraces.

overlooks built out into the river. Upstream from the center of downtown, new apartments on the river have boat docks.

Bob Beckley left Milwaukee in 1985 to become the dean of the school of architecture at the University of Michigan, but he had set in motion a major urban design project that took some 30 years to implement.

On warm summer days in downtown Milwaukee, there are boats moving up and down the river and people eating and drinking on the terraces. The walkways are close to the street level, making them part of the downtown circulation system, and as 4.4 shows, they have become rentable commercial frontages.

The city's investment has been important in making the walkway happen, but the driving force has been the building owners. As we anticipated, back in 1981, a second frontage along the river turns out to be a valuable financial asset.

Midtown Omaha

In 2001, I was part of a consulting team put together by HDR, the big international architecture and engineering firm, to prepare the Destination Midtown urban design plan for Omaha, Nebraska. HDR had started in Omaha and still has its management office there. Another national company, Mutual of Omaha, had its headquarters in the midtown area, a prominent office tower with the company's logo at the top. Mutual also controlled a large swath of land around their building which they were using for employee parking. Their parking extended to the frontage of Turner Park, east of their building; the park at that time was little more than a green lawn with some clumps of trees (4.5).

4.5 The headquarters office complex for Mutual of Omaha is at the left of this 1997 photo, with two blocks of parking, mostly owned by Mutual, separating it from Turner Park. The park at the time was not much more than a lawn and some clumps of trees. We saw the combination of the parking lots and the park as an opportunity for a new development that could become the centerpiece for the whole of Omaha's midtown area.

Large amounts of land under a single ownership are always a potential urban design and development opportunity. We made some sketches of what might be possible and brought them to a meeting with Mutual. We saw Turner Park as a key element for any new development on Mutual's parking lots because it would give the new buildings a design focus and a foreground for views across the city to downtown. We proposed that a redesigned park would be shared between the City and Mutual, with a grand entrance drive which would be partly in the park and partly on Mutual's property. We drew this drive as a circle. It would be framed by new buildings which would look across the park to the downtown skyline. After some skepticism, Mutual decided to go ahead with a project on their land, and, once they had decided to do it, courageously developed it all at one time. In the completed project, called Midtown Crossing and designed by Cope Linder Architects, our proposal for a circular drive became an ellipse, bringing an enlarged Turner Park into the heart of Mutual's development, where it is surrounded by apartment buildings, with shops and restaurants on their ground floors (4.6). The entrance drive opens into a large space with a strong identity (4.7) and the new design includes a stage at the southern end of Turner Park, just visible in the distance in this photo, which has turned it into an important event space (4.8).

The 15-acre, 1-million-square-foot development includes 220,000 square feet of retail space, 297 condominiums, 196 rental apartments, a 132-room Westin Element Hotel, a multiplex cinema, and 3,000 garage spaces, with a new public streetscape and the complete redesign and renovation of Turner Park.

The Destination Midtown plan was not just about what should happen to one set of properties. It also included designs for street realignments

4.6 Midtown Crossing, developed by Mutual of Omaha, now includes an enlarged Turner Park which has become a major event space. The park is the foreground for apartments that look across it toward Omaha's downtown skyline. The architects for the buildings and the open space were Cope Linder Architects.

4.7 Inside Midtown Crossing's oval entrance drive. The enlarged Turner Park is on the right.

4.8 Looking across Turner Park toward the stage with the skyline of downtown Omaha in the distance.

and proposed a streetcar connection between downtown and midtown, as well as for reinforcing neighborhood commercial districts and adding a substantial component of affordable housing, mostly to be created by renovating existing buildings. Each of these components has required its own implementation strategy. The streetcar, running from the Riverfront Park downtown past Midtown Crossing to the University of Nebraska medical complex at the western end of midtown, is only just now becoming an actual project.

The part of the story involving Mutual of Omaha has an interesting sequel. Twenty years later, Mutual, post-pandemic, has many of its office employees working from home for part of the week. The company has decided that it only needs about half its current office space. With many of their midtown office buildings becoming outdated, Mutual has made a deal with the City of Omaha to develop a new office tower on the site of the old central library, a prominent downtown location. Even with only half Mutual's current office space, the 44-story new tower will be by far the tallest building downtown. Other parts of the agreement include the city taking over the maintenance of Turner Park from Mutual and buying the three parking garages that support Midtown Crossing. Mutual will entertain proposals from developers for their remaining land and office buildings. The completion of the streetcar proposed as part of the Destination Midtown plan, with frequent service linking all Omaha's central locations, is considered an important element in making the redevelopment of Mutual's old office space feasible.

Implementation strategies

Each of these projects began with a very general urban design idea. In Nashville, it was an expectation that the city should have a public square, a concept with a long history but an actual public square no longer existed. In Milwaukee, the idea of turning the river frontage into a public amenity also had a long history but nothing had been done to make it happen. In Omaha, we knew that the Destination Midtown plan needed midtown to have an identifiable centerpiece and saw the combination of Turner Park and Mutual's parking lots as a way to make such a place happen.

The next step each time was to present a visualization of what could be possible. Our little report for Nashville Metro showed with sketches that the parking lot in front of the courthouse could be transformed into an attractive space. The studio at the University of Wisconsin Milwaukee was a demonstration of what could happen if the riverfront were lined with public promenades. The sketches we showed in our meeting with Mutual reminded them of the real-estate potential of their extensive parking lots.

Each project also needed a funding mechanism to move it from idea to reality. In Nashville, the construction of a 1,000-car underground parking garage, which would need a roof in any case, made the money needed for the park on top a small fraction of the combined projects. In Milwaukee, the development of a second frontage along the river had a real-estate value. The city's timely subsidy for the construction of walkways and bulkheads helped catalyze the project, which depended on participation by many building owners. In Omaha, our proposals also had a real-estate value, and the city's willingness to make Turner Park part of the project made the location much more marketable. Mutual's development is discussed again in Chapter 9 as the first example of Omaha's Civic Place Districts.

5

PRESERVING EXISTING URBAN DESIGNS

It is now well-accepted that landmark buildings of historical importance or outstanding architecture should be preserved, and the principle has been extended to districts which contain a group of buildings which are historic or have a consistent architectural character. However, maintaining an existing urban design is beyond the objectives of historic preservation as usually defined and requires a different kind of preservation to maintain the original organizing concept even when the kinds of buildings have changed.

Preserving the Cleveland Group Plan in the 1980s and 1990s: In 1982, Hunter Morrison, the director of planning in Cleveland, asked me to review the design of the Sohio Building then being planned for a prominent site on Cleveland's Public Square. Downtown Cleveland has an inventory of neo-classical buildings dating from the City Beautiful Movement at the turn of the last century and continuing up through the 1930s. These buildings establish a distinctive urban design character. Cleveland's famous reform mayor, Tom L. Johnson, had commissioned three architects well known for their work on civic buildings, Daniel Burnham, John Carrère, and Arnold Brunner, to propose a civic center for Cleveland. Their design, usually referred to as the Cleveland Group Plan, was completed in 1903. As shown in this appropriately smoky rendering (5.1), a central mall along a north-south axis began at the courthouse and library, which are the twin buildings at the south end, and extended to a railroad station over the tracks next to Lake Erie at the northern end. The railway station was never built, but two more near-twin neo-classical buildings, the City Hall and the County building, were built as planned at the northern end of the mall on a bluff-overlooking Lake Erie. The Cleveland Public Auditorium and the headquarters of the Board of Education were other neo-classical buildings along the east side of the mall. The center line of the park space was clearly defined by a war memorial located in a plaza in front of the library and courthouse.

I sat down with Hunter in his office to look through the Sohio Building working drawings, which were already close to being finished. Superior Avenue and Euclid Avenue converge at Public Square. Euclid comes in on a diagonal and ends, while Superior is on the downtown grid and, at the time, continued on through the Square.[1] The architects of the

DOI: 10.4324/9781003384106-6

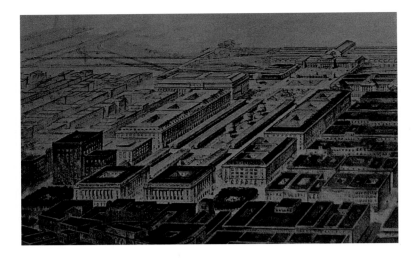

5.1 A drawing of the 1903 Cleveland Group Plan designed by architects Daniel Burnham, John Carrère, and Arnold Brunner as a civic center for the city. Much of this plan was implemented through the 1930s and generations of decision-makers have worked to preserve the original urban design as times have changed and the scale of new buildings has become much larger.

Sohio Building, Helmuth Obata and Kassabaum from St. Louis, had made the converging geometry of the two avenues their main design concern. Their tower folded in the middle, so part of it was aligned with Euclid Avenue and part with Superior. There was a lower building using the same geometry which resulted in a residual open space facing Public Square. The Square consisted of four large park blocks and didn't need any additional open space. Just north of the proposed building were the twin neo-classical buildings at the southern end of the Cleveland Group Plan that defined the central axis along the mall. The tower was in the middle of the Sohio property, but conspicuously not on the centerline established by the Group Plan, despite the expectation of symmetry that was the clear organizing principle of Cleveland's most important design element. The view of the tower from the north, through the space between the library and the courthouse, was always going to look wrong if the tower were not on the mall's axis of symmetry. It is not as if the architects knowingly set off their tower in opposition to the centerline of the Group Plan. It was clear they had just ignored it.

I said that it looked to me that the Plaza adding additional open space to the Square was the product of design decisions made about the tower, and the plans were too far along to make it possible to change it without in effect starting over. However, it might not be too late to adjust the width of the parking garage behind the tower and move the whole office building over, so the Superior Avenue frontage of the tower aligned with the axis of the Group Plan. Hunter picked up his phone and got us into see the mayor that afternoon.

We met with Mayor George Voinovich in his very grand office suite in City Hall, which made the New York City mayor's office look like a country cottage in comparison. Hunter introduced me and explained that we had been looking at the plans for the Sohio Building and that there were changes we thought needed to be made.

PRESERVING EXISTING URBAN DESIGNS

"What would you do in my place?" the mayor asked.

I replied that I knew he came from a family of architects and engineers so what I would do might also be something that he would agree was important. I explained the problem of relating the tower to the Cleveland Group Plan.

The contract documents for the Sohio Building were close to completion, which made it difficult to suggest any changes, and I knew that the building was important for the city's economy. However, I thought there was a way to fix the problem without jeopardizing the project.

The Sohio parking garage, between the tower and the Cleveland Arcade next door, was not closely connected to the structure of the main building. The garage was likely to be scheduled for construction toward the end of the building process, so there would be time to redesign it. By changing the garage, it would be possible to move the whole of the rest of the design to align the tower with the city's most important urban design composition, without changing any fundamental part of the design except the foundation plan. I made a scraggly looking sketch that explained this idea. Mayor Voinovich decided that the change was worth discussing with Sohio. With the mayor's backing, Hunter was able to negotiate the move, although it can't have been easy (5.2). Sohio later merged with BP America, which moved out of the building in 1998. The building is now known as 200 Public Square.

After this experience, Hunter found a way to prevent a similar situation from happening again. He persuaded the city to extend the jurisdiction of the Art Commission to include approving developments in much of downtown Cleveland. I then sat down with Linda Henrichsen, who was in charge of planning for downtown, and we worked out a series of maps that used a vocabulary of setback and build-to lines, height limits, and placements for future buildings in highly visible locations. We also identified locations for public open space, and mapped asterisks at the end of vistas which should have special design attention. These diagrams and accompanying text showed design issues the city considered important in advance of any development proposal (5.3).[2] Versions of these maps, using a more traditional illustrative plan presentation, were included in the Cleveland Civic Vision Downtown Plan, published in 1989.

The design for the Society Bank Corporation tower, a tall building designed by Cesar Pelli, is like the Sohio Building, far larger than any structure contemplated in the original design of the Cleveland Group Plan. It occupies a position fronting on both Public Square and the Mall, with the bank's initial brownstone building on Public Square renovated and preserved and with a new hotel developed along the Mall next door. The original bank building was designed by John Wellborn Root, Daniel Burnham's partner, and opened in 1890. Pelli's design for the new bank tower carries the color of the old building across

68 PRESERVING EXISTING URBAN DESIGNS

5.2 This view of the twin buildings at the south end of the Mall shows that the tower of the Sohio Building – now 200 Public Square – aligns with the central axis of the Mall, a change from the original design where the tower would have been farther to the right in this view and the termination of the Mall axis would have been the building's parking garage.

PRESERVING EXISTING URBAN DESIGNS

the lower part of its base, and parts of the new façade are set back to match horizontal lines in the adjacent lower building. The tower is also modulated vertically to appear slimmer and to recognize its position as a pivot between Public Square and the Mall.[3] The whole Mall side of the tower is set back to mirror the setback from the Mall at the Board of Education Building (now the Drury Plaza Hotel) directly opposite Next to the side of the tower facing the Mall, the façade of the Marriott Hotel is in scale with earlier Mall buildings; the tower for the rooms is back on the other side of the block. The original bank building was completely renovated and the two lobbies joined. The parking for this project is a garage under the adjacent block of the Mall, city property, which helped urban design concerns to play

PRESERVING EXISTING URBAN DESIGNS

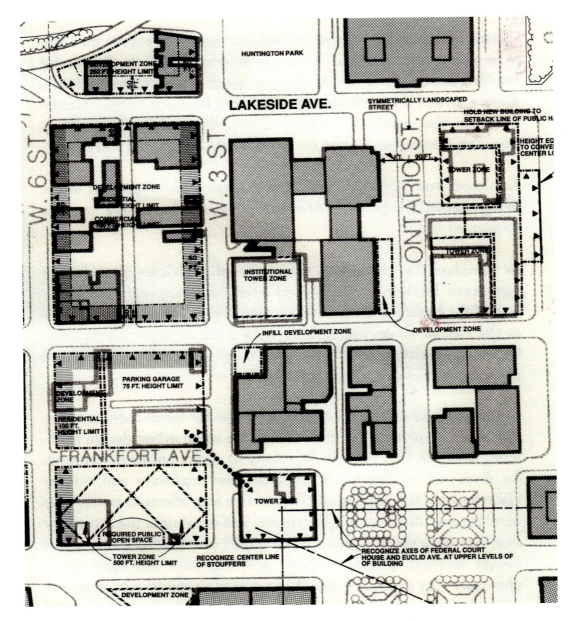

5.3 This is an example of the guidelines prepared by Cleveland's City Planning Department to serve as criteria for the Art Commission when it reviewed proposals in downtown Cleveland. The guidelines use a vocabulary of build-to and setback lines, height limits, and building placements. The blocks at the left have a build-to line and a setback above 50 feet which permits additional height up to the limit of the floor area. In this diagram, the recently completed Key Tower in the upper right-hand corner of Public Square is shown as an existing building.

such a significant part in the project.[4] Society Bank Corporation and Key Bank Corporation, a bank based in Albany, New York, merged to become Key Corporation in 1994. Their Cleveland building is now known as Key Tower.

I watched Cesar Pelli make a presentation to the Cleveland Art Commission to explain how his building met their urban design guidelines. Pelli was such a brilliant presenter that I think the Art Commission would have approved just about anything he showed them, but Pelli understood the issues of relating his building to the context created by Public Square and the Cleveland Group Plan and did work with them. The result was a much taller building than was shown in the original Group Plan rendering, but it does follow the Plan's building placement and acknowledges its design context far more completely than the Sohio Building.

The expansion of the Cleveland Public Library was another of the buildings approved by the Art Commission in accordance with the guidelines the planning department had drawn. The guidelines required that the new building be clearly separated from the iconic original building, because it is one of the two almost-twin buildings that frame 3rd Street at the south end of the Mall. The guidelines also required that the design of the new building recognizes both the library and the formidably neo-classical Federal Reserve Building directly across 6th Street by using compatible materials and by holding to the front property line at its four corners. The architect, Malcolm Holzman of Hardy Holzman Pfeiffer Associates, found a way to follow the guidelines and still design a modern building, completed in 1998, that met the library's program requirements. The building is a ten-story tower, oval in plan and faced in glass, but it also has four subsidiary elements faced in stone, six stories high, which come right out to the sidewalks at the corners of the building. The effect is of a glass building bursting through the restraints of traditional architecture (5.4). There is a landscaped outdoor reading garden between the old library and the new extension, with the connections between the old and new libraries made via an underground concourse. From Superior Avenue, the new library fits well into the street wall established by earlier buildings (5.5). The building demonstrates how design guidelines can create a productive relationship between the existing context and the specific architecture of an individual building.

Preserving the Cleveland Group Plan Today: This current aerial view of the Cleveland Mall (5.6) shows Cesar Pelli's Key Tower as the hinge between Public Square on the lower left and the Mall. The 200 Public Square Building is on the lower right and you can see how its tower terminates the south end of the Mall. The Stokes Building, the extension of the central library, is to the right of the library building, separated from the original structure by the Reading Garden.

Back in 1964, a Convention Center had been built underground beneath the central segment of the Mall, connected to the adjacent

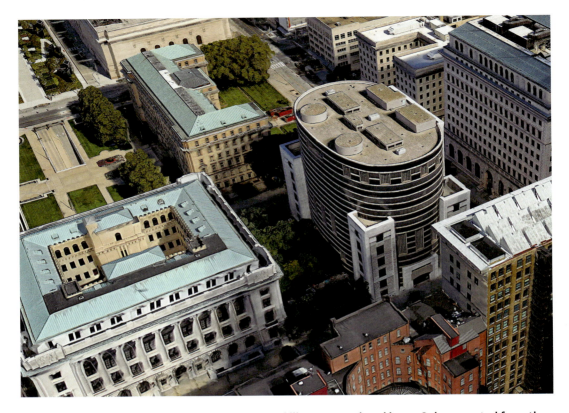

5.4 The Louis Stokes wing of the Cleveland central library, completed in 1998, is separated from the original building by a landscaped reading garden, with the connection between the two buildings made via an underground concourse, following the official guidelines by keeping the design of the original building separate and intact. Another guideline, holding the corners of the new building to the street line and recognizing the surrounding neo-classical stone buildings, has also been followed in an interesting way. The four corners are stone architectural vignettes six-story high, while the building itself is a ten-story oval glass tower. The effect is of a modern building bursting through the constraints of traditional architecture. The architect was Malcolm Holzman of the firm Hardy Holzman Pfeiffer Associates.

Public Auditorium. The completely rebuilt Huntington Convention Center replaced the old convention center in 2013. While it is also largely underneath the middle section on the Mall, its green roof ramps up to cover an entrance hall on the north. In the aerial view, you can see the shadow cast by the raised section of the Mall on Lakeside Avenue. It is no longer possible to stand at the south end of the Mall and see the whole space, although it still reads as green with no buildings visible at the end. On the west side of the middle section of the Mall is the Global Center for Health Innovation which mirrors the height and placement of the Civic Auditorium facing the Mall on the other side. A new convention center hotel at Lakeside Avenue and the west side of the Mall, still under construction in this view, creates a kind of symmetry with the new scale established by the Key Tower at the south end. Two more almost-twin buildings dating

5.5 This photo shows how the six-story stone corners of the Louis Stokes Wing relate the building to the street wall of masonry-faced buildings along Superior Avenue, although the main part of the building is an oval ten-story building faced in glass.

from the original design, the City Hall in the upper right-hand corner of the photo and the County Courthouse Building just visible in the upper left, frame what is now a separate green space. There are plans to connect this segment of the Mall across the railway tracks to new buildings on the lakefront.

The original Group Plan design, while greatly transformed, remains a powerful presence for generations of decision-makers, as shown by the difficult and expensive process of building a modern convention center mostly underground. The Mall is still seen as an organizing concept, and, if it is extended to the Lake, would give its design a completion that it has not had up until now.

Preserving the Country Club Plaza District in Kansas City: In the mid-1980s, I was working for Kansas City Redevelopment Authority as an urban design consultant and John Laney, the Deputy City

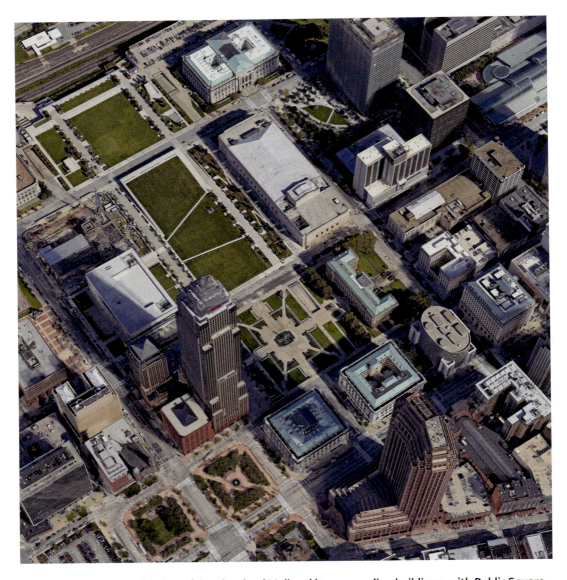

5.6 This is a current aerial view of the Cleveland Mall and its surrounding buildings, with Public Square in the lower left-hand corner and the Mall in the center. The Key Tower occupies a hinge point between Public Square and the buildings facing the Mall. The 200 Public Square building is on the lower right and it is clear in this view how the tower is located to recognize the central design axis of the Mall. The Louis Stokes Wing and its Reading Garden are on the right of the original library building. Just visible in the top left of the photo is the County Courthouse, with the City Hall, its near twin, in a comparable position on the other side of the Mall. The central section of the Mall was ramped up from south to north in 2013 to cover a completely redesigned convention center which had been under this part of the Mall since 1964. It is still a continuous green area, but it is no longer possible to stand at the south end of the Mall and see the whole space. There are plans to connect the northernmost portion of the Mall to buildings at the lakefront, at a lower elevation across the railway tracks. Despite changes in the scale of the surrounding buildings and changes to the Mall itself, its design is still a major shaping force in the development of downtown Cleveland.

Manager, asked me to conduct a planning study for the Country Club Plaza District. A developer had purchased a parcel of land just east of the historic Plaza retail area and announced plans for a 40-story building. If the intent was to build up interest and excitement about the proposed building, it succeeded, but not in a way that the developer would have wanted. People in the residential neighborhoods around the Plaza were not enthusiastic about the possibility that they would open the front doors of their suburban houses and garden apartment buildings and be confronted by a 40-story office tower. Community activists soon recognized that the zoning could permit many more similar buildings. They put pressure on City Hall to do something about this.

I worked with Judy Hansen, chief of the planning and urban design division of the City Planning and Development Department. Judy and I decided that the Plaza District was far too large to have manageable community meetings that could accommodate everyone interested, and we marked out four quadrants of the Plaza District which would be sub-planning areas where I could conduct smaller community discussions.

Early in the process, a hostile editorial appeared in the Kansas City Star. I no longer remember exactly what it said, but the general tone was: who is this consultant from New York and what horrors will he be inflicting on the Plaza neighborhoods? People recognized immediately that the author of the editorial was someone who lived in an apartment building near the Art Museum in one of the Plaza-planning areas. The president of the Parks and Recreation Board, Anita Gorman, arranged a meeting for Judy and me with the editorial board of the Star. I explained what I and the city were doing, and there were no more denunciations.

The Plaza as a Bowl: The Country Club Plaza retail district had been built by the J.C. Nichols Company as part of their much larger land development that consisted of whole new neighborhoods.[5] The shop buildings were designed in a picturesque Spanish style, with attractive fountains, landscaping, and ornamental towers. It was originally a local shopping center, but by the mid-1980s, it had grown and evolved into a major retail destination, with a carefully chosen group of stores that catered to people with discretionary income, plus movie theaters and a large selection of restaurants. The retail had always been intended for shoppers arriving by car, and, over the years, the large numbers of car spaces needed were accommodated by putting cars on rooftops or, underground, or in garages hidden behind shopfronts. While parking was easy to find, there were no at-grade parking lots like those that surround so many retail destinations. South of the shopping district, across Brush Creek, the Nichols Company had developed hotels and apartment buildings on higher land mostly at about 10 or 11 stories, and there were comparable buildings north of the Plaza as well. When I showed slides of the Plaza District to facilitate discussion in community meetings, I said that the Plaza and the buildings around it had become an unusually successful urban design. I compared it to a bowl. The low-rise retail buildings were at the bottom of the bowl and the taller buildings on the rising terrain around it were the sides, as shown in this view (5.7).

This design was worth conserving and it could be lost with the wrong kind of new development. If the base of the bowl were redeveloped to buildings as tall as the sides, the design would be lost. If the buildings on the sides became out of scale with the prevailing height of the sides of the bowl, the design would be compromised. This did not mean that there should not be new development, just that whatever was added should relate to what was already there. The idea that the physical form of the Plaza District was like a bowl resonated with the people who came to the meetings. They had not thought of it that way, but it conformed to their experiences.

Brush Creek as a River: At the time of these meetings, Brush Creek ran through the Plaza District as a trickle of water at the bottom of a wide concrete drainage ditch. In 1977, there had been a disastrous flash flood along Brush Creek which killed 25 people, some caught unawares in the Plaza District and some in the predominantly African American neighborhoods on the city's east side. There was also

5.7 The low-rise retail at the Country Club Plaza in Kansas City is surrounded by taller buildings, an urban design composition which can be described as a bowl: the retail district is at the base and the taller surrounding buildings form the side. If portions of the retail village were to be rebuilt as towers, the urban design composition would be lost. Public support for the "bowl concept" has helped to keep it intact. It is now protected by a height limit in the Kansas City zoning ordinance.

massive property damage. By the time I was working on the Plaza plan, the U.S. Army Corps of Engineers was developing a redesign for Brush Creek. I met with their engineering consultants. They showed me a plan that would construct what they called break-away dams along the Creek. The dams would make the Creek look like a river, with water filling the space between the banks all the time. In the event of a flood, the additional water pressure would cause the dams to open up and the flood waters would flow through. I could see that this would be a great way to improve the design of the Plaza District. I spoke about the project at meetings and drew maps showing how many places would become waterfront property, instead of looking out on a concrete channel. The Corps of Engineers plan was accepted by the city and implemented. There was another bad flood in 1998, with some of the problem caused by low-lying bridges which became flooded and also caught debris, causing waters to back up. There have been modifications to improve how Brush Creek manages flooding since then, but it still looks like a river, and it is still an amenity.

The Plan and Its Afterlife: The neighborhood meetings all voted in favor of the plan I had worked out with them, and I prepared the plan document with the staff of the City Planning and Development Department. *The Plaza Urban Design and Development Plan* was adopted and published in 1989. The developer who had set off the whole process turned out not to control anything like enough property to construct a 40-story building under the existing zoning and the site ended up being a group of garden apartments. I had talked with Lynn McCarthy, the president and CEO of the Nichols Company, about placing a height limit in the city's zoning ordinance on the Country Club Plaza retail buildings. He said that the company would never agree to this, and he was certain they had enough influence on the City Council to make sure it could not happen. The city staff agreed with this assessment. We could write about a height limit on the retail district as part of the plan, but we couldn't get a zoning change through the City Council.

McCarthy assured me that the Nichols Company was now employee-owned, and he and the other people who worked there would never do anything to spoil the character of their development. At the time we were speaking, the Nichols Company was losing many millions of dollars it had put into a development in St. Petersburg, Florida, and the management was soon forced to sell a controlling interest in their whole company to New York investors, Allen & Company. In 2002, McCarthy himself was sentenced to five years' probation for defrauding the Nichols Company from 1986 through 1995.[6]

Somehow the center of the Country Club Plaza has survived as a low-rise district, and the recent, taller buildings along 47th Street to the west are still more-or-less in keeping with earlier taller buildings that formed the edges of the original design composition. In 2015, the city prepared a new, but less detailed, area plan that included the Country

Club retail district and the development around it. People from the community came to the meetings with copies of the 1989 plan and succeeded in getting its more specific provisions incorporated in the new plan – including the bowl concept which set the building height recommendations in relation to the Country Club Plaza, and the maps that supported development in specific areas.

The community had remembered the Plaza Urban Design and Development Plan, even when the official planners had apparently forgotten it. In 2019, the Kansas City Council voted to impose a 45-foot height limit over the Plaza's shopping district.[7] Implementing this urban design provision took 30 years, but given the current retailing revolution, it is probably still an important way to preserve the original design.

Implementation strategies

Preserving an urban design means preserving as many of its underlying principles as possible, even when the conditions that produced the original buildings have changed. These principles can be translated into objective criteria like height limits, setbacks, and build-to lines, which can be incorporated in a zoning district or used as criteria for design review.

People know when they like a place and understand what makes a place likable. Keeping Cleveland's green Mall open and maintaining the axial symmetry were well understood as basic elements of the city's character. Sometimes, the explanation of what makes an urban design successful can be as simple as it was for Kansas City's Plaza District. The district was designed according to a clear concept of street level retail in small buildings, and their low height was the most significant element, even more than the "Spanish" style that characterized the earlier buildings. Keeping the shopping district in its original low-rise configuration, with the parking well concealed, was the critical urban design consideration.

6

CHANGING REGULATIONS TO PREVENT SUBURBAN SPRAWL

What is called suburban sprawl is not the result of market forces; it is primarily the product of three obsolete regulatory concepts: the blindness of regulations to environmental conditions, the minimum lot sizes in the zoning regulations which make all the house lots across a large area the same size, and the mapping of narrow strips zoned for commercial uses along suburban highways. The real estate market then responded to the rules set by local governments by creating a suburban development template that has become the default suburban design across the entire United States. Farms and woodlands have been flattened and re-engineered to prepare them for development. Regular patterns of residential subdivision extend for miles in every direction, with each house similar to its neighbors and on the same-sized lot. Suburban highways are lined with signs and parking lots for strip shopping centers, fast food franchises, filling stations, motels, and small office buildings. People have adjusted their lifestyle to fit this now-established pattern, where almost every trip outside the house requires a car. Many people like it and have accepted its problems as inevitable. But turning an entire landscape into house lots, highways, and parking lots has made whole communities vulnerable to flooding after a heavy rainfall. A highway lined with businesses which make drivers turn into each separate parking lot is a recipe for traffic congestion. And with shopping, schools, and work all reached by car, there are congested rush-hours morning and evening every weekday. Saturday, when everyone runs errands, can have the worst traffic of all.

Wildwood rejects the usual suburban growth

People living in the western part of St. Louis County liked where they lived, but they did not like the way the usual development template was transforming their community. They wanted to take control themselves. In February 1995, after a long political campaign, they seceded from the county in a special election to create Wildwood, a new city covering 67 square miles. Sixty-one percent of area residents turned out for a referendum on incorporation, and 61 percent of those voting approved it.

That August, I received a phone call from Barbara Foy, one of 16 local leaders appointed to an interim city council. In September, Wildwood would officially become a city, and, as soon as it did, the county

DOI: 10.4324/9781003384106-7

zoning and subdivision ordinances would no longer apply. The local home builders had agreed not to fight a three-month moratorium, but then they wanted to start up again. Barbara's question: "Can you help us create a new zoning ordinance in three months?"

I said I would call her back and called Brian Blaesser, a development and land-use lawyer with Robinson & Cole in Boston. I had worked with him before, and I knew he could deal creatively with unusual situations. His reaction was that three months was not an impossible deadline for a new zoning ordinance as long as many of the provisions followed the county's existing ordinances – as they should anyway to avoid nonconforming uses. If the community wanted to create controversial new requirements, he added, it would need a master plan to document the reasons for the changes.

I went out to Wildwood at the end of August to meet with some of the leaders of the three-year battle to incorporate. They had first come together as part of a coalition that successfully opposed a third metropolitan ring road that would have run through the center of their community. They moved on to considering a separate government after concluding that county officials would continue to ignore their complaints about poor development practices.

They gave me a tour of some of the problem areas in their community. Developers had been stripping away trees, carting away topsoil, and bulldozing hillsides into valleys. Because there was no regional stormwater management system, accelerated runoff was eroding other properties further down the watershed, washing away stream banks, and undermining bridges and streets. In several places, underground sewer mains and electrical conduit had been exposed by erosion.

These problems had all been photographed, mapped, and presented to the county commission – without any effect on county policies (6.1).

6.1 One of the photographs taken by Wildwood residents to document the erosion taking place because of St. Louis County's ill-judged development policies. This photo, like many of the others, was taken by Maryanne E. Simmons.

Along the Old Manchester Road, in the historic center of the community, the county had been making changes from residential to commercial zoning, with results that looked ominously like an extension of the strip development along the same road in neighboring communities to the east. Despite two years of meetings with county staff to draft new plans for this area, the county had gone right on granting zoning changes outside of anything contemplated in the on-going discussions with the community.

The county was also planning to widen many of the local roads to manage future traffic congestion that the county's traffic engineers saw as inevitable.

The problems, as everyone in the room understood, came from official policies. They added up to a kind of urban design strategy, but one based on decisions made without sufficient understanding of what the effects would be. I told the leaders of the new community they were right that a first step had to be changes in the zoning and subdivision regulations, which could allow them to add environmental safeguards. They could keep existing residential densities but did not have to keep uniform minimum lot sizes, and there could also be a mixed-use, walkable town center as an alternative to the conventional commercial strip. I also thought that more compact development, with stronger internal street systems, could ease traffic congestion and reduce the need to widen highways.

However, as a designer, I would need back-up on legal matters from a lawyer who sympathized with these objectives. I told the community leaders about Brian Blaesser and his qualifications from working with planners across the country to revise zoning regulations and told them Brian thought he could work within their deadline. I also relayed Brian's judgment that these kinds of changes would need the support of a well-documented master plan.

A master plan requires basic findings of fact, about the natural landscape, historic sites, traffic, the location and condition of sewers and other infrastructure such as the water supply, the location and condition of roads and bridges, the availability of urban services such as fire and police protection, and information about the school district. Selecting a consulting firm to gather this background information would normally take more time than the three months they had available to do the work itself. As time and budget were both so limited, I proposed that some of the people around the table participate in gathering data for the master plan. I said I could tell them what was needed and teach them how to find the information while we were putting the plan together. In addition to Brian Blaesser, we would also need the continued counsel of Daniel Vogel, the lawyer who had taken Wildwood through the secession and incorporation processes and would now serve as the city attorney. I could suggest a traffic consultant, and I would need their help in identifying someone to advise us on the local erosion issues. If all these parts came together, I could meet their deadline with a draft master plan, and

Brian had undertaken to identify and redraft the parts of the county regulations that would need to be changed on the same schedule.

Gathering Information for the Master Plan: Research by high-powered, motivated citizens turned out to be an excellent way to unlock data from bureaucracies in the school district and the county, and from state agencies like the transportation department. For environmental advice, Stephanie Lickerman, chair of the newly formed Wildwood Planning and Zoning Commission – and an adept user of the Internet – located David Hammer, a professor of environmental science at the University of Missouri in Columbia. She also persuaded the regional research institute at the University of Southern Illinois at Edwardsville to set up Wildwood's geographic information system at an exceptionally reasonable cost, using data files provided by the county as well as their own resources.

"That's a classic," David Hammer kept saying on his first tour of Wildwood as he saw textbook results of stripped vegetation, bulldozing, blocked drainage ways, and improperly sized and placed detention basins. Hammer noted that Wildwood, located in the foothills of the Ozarks some 25 miles from St. Louis, was much more sensitive to erosion than the alluvial plain nearer the city. Development practices that might be acceptable elsewhere in the county were certainly not working here.

Walter Kulash, a transportation planner with the Orlando firm of Glatting Jackson Kercher Anglin Lopez Rinehart, came to Wildwood and we drove with him along the city's narrow, back-country roads. Would they need to be widened?

After reviewing the traffic counts Sue Cullinane had extracted from county and state offices, the county's population projections, and the master plan principles we were discussing, Walter concluded that we could accommodate expected traffic growth on existing roads, if safety improvements were made in some locations and new developments had strong internal street systems, a requirement which could be written into the subdivision ordinance. This conclusion meshed with David Hammer's advice against disrupting the natural landscape with the regrading needed for road widenings.

Midway through the planning process, Wildwood hired Joseph Vujnich, a county planner well respected by local citizens, to be its director of planning and parks. Joe and I went to see officials at the water and sewer district. We learned that there were no plans to add a stormwater system to the Wildwood area. Also, sewage treatment systems were close to capacity and there were no plans to extend sewers westward beyond a boundary located approximately at Highway 109, which runs north-south through the center of Wildwood.

Working Out the Master Plan Design Concepts: I held an all-day meeting with Joe and the community leaders at the home of one of them, Dennis Tacchi, an architect. We spread out some of Joe's maps from the county and some of Dennis's tracing paper on his dining room table.

Much of Wildwood had been zoned for three-acre lots, a decision made when St. Louis County first adopted development regulations in 1965. Uniform three-acre zoning is not the ideal way either to preserve the landscape or to organize new development, but it would be extremely difficult if not impossible to change it, and certainly very time-consuming. Three acres were usually enough for a workable septic system and David Hammer considered building houses at this density to be manageable within Wildwood's landscape. West of Highway 109, where there were no plans to extend the sewers, it seemed a sensible public policy to affirm the existing zoning in the master plan. We drew a line on the map which meant a policy of no zoning changes west of that line.

There were two big parks within Wildwood's boundaries on the west side of Highway 109, Babler State Park and the Rockwoods Reservation. We drew a wildlife corridor connecting the two, with additional wildlife corridor connections from the parks to the Missouri River on the north and the Meramec River on the south. This policy meant that any development within the corridor should be designed to allow unimpeded movement of wildlife. As the land was zoned for a maximum of one house for every three acres, it should be possible to cluster development so that such a corridor could be maintained.

East of Highway 109, some land had already been built out at three-acre zoning; in many other places, the county had approved subdivisions with half-acre or quarter-acre lots, and higher densities in planned unit developments. It would make sense to round out these partly realized zoning patterns, where they could be managed without creating new erosion problems. We drew some more lines on the map.

No one wanted to see the commercial strip zoning in adjoining Ellisville spread along the Old Manchester Road through the middle of Wildwood, which was where the early settlers had identified the flattest and most buildable land and located their first small towns. We also knew that, if Wildwood's master plan were too conservative, it would be attacked by developers as anti-growth. Many of the people in the room were familiar with New Urbanist planning ideas, and there was the beginning of a Duany/Plater-Zyberk-designed new town in St. Charles County farther to the west. I suggested that we could satisfy the demands for growth by planning a higher-density mixed-use center on the north side of the Old Manchester Road up to Highway 109 where the most buildable land was located. This was not the kind of density the homebuilders would be asking for, but it was definitely pro-growth. We delineated the boundaries of a town center, a mixed-use district that would pull together several widely separated commercial re-zonings that the county had already granted and would also permit residential densities higher, and lot sizes smaller, than anywhere else in Wildwood. The town center would have a main street for shops and offices, and it would be a place where people could park their cars and walk. There would be apartments and townhouses so that young people and the elderly could continue to live in the community.

By the end of the day, we had agreed on the basic policies that should be delineated in the master plan. I had a good feeling about the meeting. I thought we had a real consensus and not just some people sitting quietly and keeping their reservations to themselves, which can definitely happen in community meetings (6.2).

Preparing the New Regulations: David Hammer worked with Brian Blaesser and his colleagues at Robinson & Cole to create environmental safeguards tailored to Wildwood's ecology, regulations that ended up being part of the new subdivision ordinance. Brian and Dan Vogel – with some back seat driving from me – restructured the other land-use laws. At Brian's suggestion, they added a grading ordinance and a tree-preservation ordinance, both necessary to prevent developers from bulldozing sites before they came to the city for approval. I worked with them to bring the zoning map into conformity with the master plan policies that we had all agreed on.

We had started work in September. By early December, drafts of both a master plan and revised development regulations were ready for public discussion. With draft documents in hand, and Christmas approaching, it was possible to extend the development moratorium to cover the public approvals process. The master plan and the new development regulations were adopted by the new Wildwood City Council in February 1996. From then on, anyone planning a new development in Wildwood has to satisfy the city that there will be no changes to natural drainage ways and steep hillsides, and must show how buildings will be kept away from sinkholes, sites of previous landslides, and any floodplains and wetlands. Other restrictions cover places with easily erodible soils and land formations susceptible to erosion.

A Specific Plan for a New Downtown: With Joe Vujnich and Dan Vogel armed with new zoning and subdivision regulations, it was time for Wildwood to prepare a specific design concept for the central mixed-use district outlined in the master plan. I suggested that the city retain Andrés Duany and Elizabeth Plater-Zyberk to lead a community-based charrette, their preferred way of working. I had participated with Andrés and Lizz on charrettes for Walton County in Florida, for downtown West Palm Beach, and for the Ocean-View neighborhood in Norfolk. I knew they would bring a team of designers to spend four or five intense days in Wildwood producing a draft master plan for the town center, working in a space in the temporary town hall where citizens could stop by and offer suggestions. At the end of every day, there would be a session open to the public which would sum up the progress so far. The event would conclude with a public presentation of the draft plan.

Wildwood negotiated an agreement with Duany Plater-Zyberk and Company (today called DPZ CoDesign). Some people were taken-aback by the contract provisions, particularly specifications about the food that would be available to the Duany Plater-Zyberk team as they worked on the project. I explained that the young staff members spent many days a year traveling to different parts of the

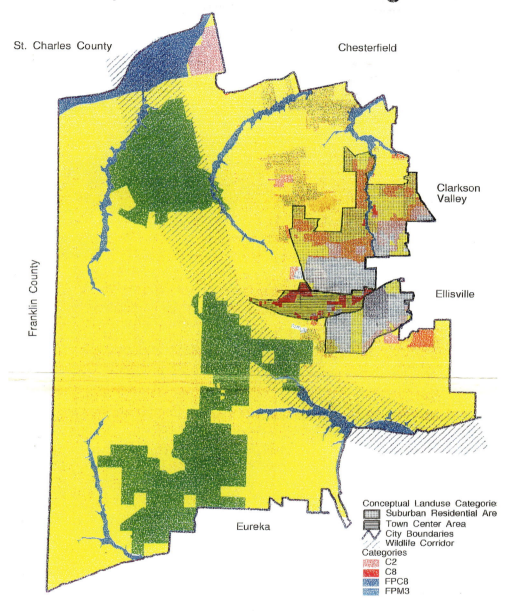

6.2 The land-use map from Wildwood's 1995 master plan. The predominant land use, shown in yellow, is the Non-Urban district which restricts development to no more than one house for every three acres, zoning which had been mapped by St. Louis County in the mid-1960s. The crescent of parallel lines denotes a Wild-Life Corridor connecting the Missouri River to the north to the Meramec River to the southeast. It runs through the Non-Urban zone and connects to Wildwood's two major park reserves. Different categories of suburban zoning are shown by textured colors. The town center zone is contained within the boat-shaped outline at the center of the map.

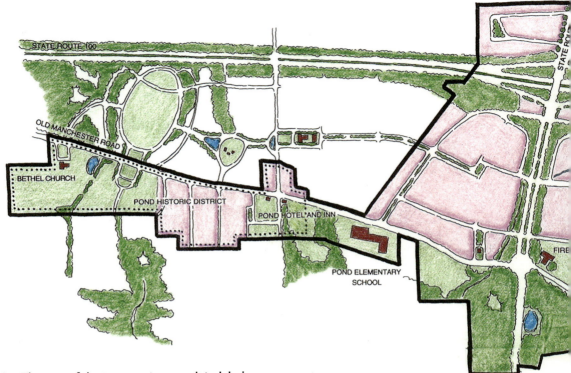

6.3 The map of the town center completed during a charrette by Duany/Plater-Zyberk and Company in 1996. The designers saw the commercial districts as developing on both sides of north-south Highway 109 in the center of the map. Real estate developers have turned out to prefer the eastern end of the town center for commercial uses, as this land is closer to existing development in Wildwood and in neighboring Ellisville and Clarkson Valley.

country to work on these kinds of projects, and they had learned that they could not expect to survive for long on a steady diet of cold-cuts and potato chips.

Andrés was to lead the team, but at the last minute had to have a minor operation. Lizz had other commitments, although she was able to clear her schedule to come to the final presentation. I ended up managing the charrette along with Tom Low from Duany Plater-Zyberk. The first thing the team did when it came to town in March 1996 was to lay out streets that fit into the original mile-square grid created when the region was first surveyed in the 19th century. The ability to map streets is, after all, one of the oldest and most accepted municipal powers.

The team had a good eye for land contours; the proposed street layout needed only minor corrections when Wildwood's engineering consultants reviewed it after the charrette. The Town Center Plan

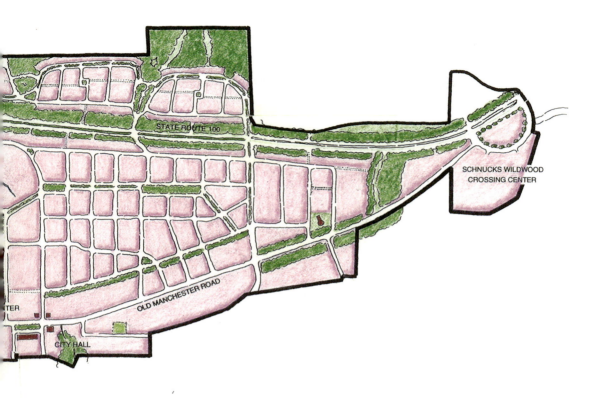

provided a clear alternative to typical suburban strip development. Stores, offices, and higher residential densities could be achieved within a street plan that looked like traditional small towns or suburbs, such as the nearby downtown of Kirkwood, Missouri. Lizz arrived in our work space just as we were putting the final touches on the drawings. She looked at the master site plan I was helping Tom render and asked: "Have you ever used those colors before?" I hadn't but Tom had, and they showed up clearly when Lizz made the slide presentation (6.3).

Soon after the charrette, Wildwood had its first election to replace the interim mayor and council appointed by the county. This election was at least partly a referendum on the master plan and the new development regulations, and backers of these policies became a big majority in the new council.

Implementing the Wildwood's Town Center Plan depends on initiatives from developers, who must make their own purchase agreements to assemble the properties they wish to develop. Andrés and Lizz were used to working with developers who already controlled the entire area they were planning. They could specify the kinds of development that would fit into their plans in a design code which was a central element of their design method. The master developers they worked with could make the design code part of the property agreement when they sold parcels of land for individual projects.

Wildwood has had to rely on its zoning regulations and its ability to build streets to implement the Town Center Plan on land divided into many separate ownerships. The Town Center Plan ran into opposition when it came up for adoption, mostly from property owners within the boundaries. Despite participation and observation during the charrette, the owners did not feel comfortable with the plan process. On Joe Vujnich's advice, the council initially adopted only a statement of design principles for the town center. Joe then took the owners through a step-by-step analysis and discussion.

Although the town-center-specific plan was eventually approved with only minor changes, final action by the council did not take place until February 1998. Joe decided to reserve actual changes to the zoning code until specific proposals came in from developers.

Implementing the Town Center Plan: Wildwood's Town Center Plan, although convincingly presented and well adapted to the terrain, was not based on building types that local developers were likely to propose and the Duany Plater-Zyberk designs were too specific to become part of zoning regulations. However, Wildwood's new zoning included an Architectural Review Board to advise the Planning Commission before it acts on any development proposals. John Guenther, an architect and one of the original group that organized the creation of Wildwood, became the chairman and the Board devoted many long sessions to working with developers to implement their projects within the plan's design concepts.

Dierberg's, a local grocery chain, had originally proposed developing a shopping center at the western end of the planned town center on steeply sloping terrain which would have required something like a 13-foot-high retaining wall behind the stores, exactly the kind of development the citizens had organized to prevent. After a lot of bluster, Dierberg's came up with an alternative site at the eastern end of the town center zone which was much easier to develop. John and the Board worked with them to design buildings that met their requirements but also would fit into the plan. Joe backed them up in the early stages by not approving the necessary streets until everyone was satisfied with the development.

Dierberg's built a conventional strip shopping center, but located on a town center street, not on the main road. The kinds of buildings that would usually be found zoned in strips along a highway are organized around a walkable street system, which is developed from what was laid out during the charrette. There is more parking than is needed, but it is what the developers insist on building. The shopping center's "pad sites" have been organized, thanks to the Architectural Review Board, so they help define Taylor Road (6.4) which is the access street connecting the Route 100 bypass on the North to the Old Manchester Road to the south. Taylor Road has a traffic signal at Route 100. There is a roundabout where Taylor Road meets the Old Manchester Road. The Old Manchester Road would have become the commercial strip if the county's way of approving development had continued.

Other development has followed the completion of Dierberg's. There are two big-box drug stores and several buildings with shops and restaurants on the ground floors and offices above. This view looking south down Fountain Place shows the ten-screen multiplex in the background. On the right is the Wildwood Hotel, on the left two buildings with restaurants on the ground floors and offices above (6.5). Looking west from the fountain on Fountain Place, the Wildwood Hotel is on your left, and, in the distance, an assisted living complex which is the first apartment building to be constructed in the town center (6.6).

In the summers, Wildwood holds a farmers market and other events in the vacant land and park space just east of the assisted living – to

6.4 The main access to the town center is Taylor Road, shown in this view, which links the Route 100 bypass on the north to the Old Manchester Road to the south – both major connectors to existing development. You are looking at two of the four "pad sites" located across a large parking lot from a shopping center anchored by a Dierberg's grocery store, just visible in the distance. The landscaped setting was suggested by Wildwood's Architectural Review Board.

6.5 Looking down Fountain Place toward the town center's Main Street. In the background are the B&B Theatres Wildwood 10. The Wildwood, a hotel, is on your right; at left are mixed-use commercial buildings.

6.6 The fountain in the center of Fountain Place. The Wildwood hotel is at left. In the distance on the right is an assisted living complex. The town center is far from being built out; much of the land is still rural.

help keep the town center on people's mental maps. There is another completed segment of Main Street in the town center to the west, off north-south Highway 109, in an area that is developing to houses on what for Wildwood is considered to be small lots, which are permitted in the town center. Eventually, the two segments of Main Street should link up, when a developer is interested and is able to persuade the intervening property owners to sell. There have been proposals that would have done this, but they have not materialized.

Wildwood built their new municipal building at what will one day be the middle of the town center. There is still a lot of open land waiting for more commercial development or higher-density housing, and well-designed and well-maintained streets and sidewalks waiting to make each new development part of the overall design.

In a later Wildwood election, two members of the original group ran against each other for mayor, splitting their vote, with the result that a third candidate was elected. He did not have the same commitment to the town center concept, and, during his administration, some small office buildings and some stores were approved outside of walking distance from the planned town center, while still in the middle of the community. Later, mayors and planning boards have gone back to the original vision, but the town center would be stronger if it could have had a l the central functions in one place.

Joe Vujnich has remained in his job through all the community's political vicissitudes, guiding developers through the approval process. There have been no new erosion problems. Joe even persuaded the Rockwood School District to build an elementary school in the center of a large subdivision of houses on the east side of the city, so that some of the children could walk to school.

Wildwood celebrated its 25th anniversary on September 21, 2021 – a year late because of the COVID-19 pandemic.[1]

Implementation strategies

Brian and I worked out the format for the master plan document, beginning with existing conditions, including David Hammer's report on Wildwood's ecology, and the statistical and mapped information gathered by the working group of community leaders. Determination of the new city's current and projected future population was especially important. We were halfway between two U.S. censuses. The county's population figure, around 23,000, was lower than our researchers thought was correct, because the county did not include residents of recently approved house lots. The future population, including only development already approved, was likely to be 30,000 by the year 2000, a revelation for many.[2] There were five master plan elements which summarized the research into existing conditions and then stated goals, objectives, and policies for each: Environment, Planning, Urban Services, Transportation, Open Space, and Recreation. As development regulations are always intended to be based on a comprehensive plan, the provisions of the master plan were essential as the support for all Wildwood's regulatory provisions.

The grading and tree-preservation ordinances, backed up by the Environmental Element in the Master Plan, have been critical in protecting Wildwood's distinctive natural environment. According to Wildwood's code, grading – that is moving earth around with a bulldozer – in preparation for any development requires a permit which will not be approved until there is also an approved plan for the development. In addition, the grading permit will not be issued until there is also a tree-preservation plan for the property. In 1996, Joe Vujnich followed up the tree planting requirement by publishing a manual to guide property owners and developers in preparing a tree-preservation plan, and in designing new landscaping and selecting and planting street trees in new developments.

Code provisions for new streets were rewritten to eliminate a specific numerical requirement for street grades. Meeting that requirement had been a significant reason why developers had been regrading entire sites. Instead, the design of streets, and their gradients, became part of the overall design of the site, to be reviewed as part of the subdivision approval process. However, any proposed street grade above 8 percent requires a complete technical review before it can be approved.

Approval of the town-center-specific plan signaled Wildwood's intention to rezone to accommodate the kinds of uses called for in the plan. The plan mapped different zones for the whole area, including commercial, workplace, and a range of neighborhood densities, which are adopted officially as development is approved. Wildwood also published a manual to show the kinds of development the city was looking for in the town center.

The Architectural Review Board has jurisdiction over all development in Wildwood except individual houses on single-family lots. The Planning Commission refers proposals to the Architectural Review Board, which advises the Planning Commission during the approval process. The Review Board has been very important in persuading developers to make their proposals conform to the Town Center Plan.

Similar strategies to those adopted in Wildwood are within reach of many other suburban communities.

7

REINVENTING SUBURBAN DEVELOPMENT

Many designers and planners admire the suburban development that took place before World War II. At least for those who could afford it, there were lively town centers and walkable neighborhoods, in contrast to the auto-dominated, spread-out suburban development that has taken over since, facilitated by a default development system which is blind to the natural environment and unduly segregates land uses and development densities. The story of Wildwood, Missouri, in the previous chapter illustrates some of the steps that people can take to counteract the worst aspects of current development by protecting the natural environment and channeling commercial uses, town houses, and apartments into a walkable town center.

But it is not possible to turn back the clock on three-quarters of a century of spread-out suburban development where the only practical way for most people to get around is by car. Some people may park their car in the Wildwood Town Center and walk to several destinations, but they will have to get back in their car to go back home or to go on to somewhere else. A few children can walk or bicycle to their elementary school in the one Wildwood neighborhood where the planning director was able to persuade the school district to build it, but most children rely on their parents or a school bus to get them to and from their classes. And, even if you live in one of Wildwood's areas where the neighborhood is walkable, having a car, or access to a ride service, is still indispensable.

Innovative suburban development at Daniel Island

Charleston, South Carolina, has a carefully preserved, walkable city center, one of the reasons it is a major tourist destination. But keeping the city of Charleston successful requires more than managing development in the center, important as that has been for both tourism and the economic viability of the region. Joseph P. Riley Jr., during his 40-year tenure as mayor, also sought opportunities to annex the surrounding suburban areas to increase the city's tax base. The city occupied 18 square miles when Riley took office, which was an increase from the size of the long-time historic center, which was only about 5 square miles. As of 2020, the city's territory was 128 square miles. The annexations have been controversial, with some arguing that

DOI: 10.4324/9781003384106-8

they have drained the historic center of resources.[1] But keeping the city small, and leaving it to be surrounded by development it could not control, would have created many more problems. So Charleston, with its strong legacy of traditional urban design, has also become the manager of large areas of spread-out suburban development.

Charleston has also used opportunities to approve a different kind of urban design when tracts of open land have come up for development. Daniel Island, 4,000 acres of fields and marsh near Charleston, was purchased by Harry Frank Guggenheim in 1947 for $70,000 (about $873,000 in current dollars). The Guggenheim family used the land for cattle ranching and as a fishing and hunting retreat. On Guggenheim's death in 1971, the ownership of Daniel Island went to a foundation he had created. As the growth of the Charleston region came closer to the Island, Joe Riley would occasionally talk to the foundation about annexation. According to Riley, they never felt the time was quite right. Finally, as plans were being completed for the Mark Clark Expressway to cross the Island, Riley went ahead with the annexation without consulting the foundation. He needed agreement from 75 percent of the landowners within the area being annexed and achieved it by including some surrounding land. He called an emergency city council meeting at 5 p.m. on December 28, 1990, and got the annexation approved.

Riley told me that the first reaction of the foundation was to take the city to court, but after they reviewed their options, they decided to accept the offer that Riley had made them, where the city would be responsible for the main roads, the water supply, and sewage treatment, and would invest in public parks and other facilities for the Island. This commitment by the city, a courageous – and hotly debated – move at the time, has created an enormous amount of taxable residential and commercial development.

With the annexation in progress, the foundation selected an advisory team to plan the development of the Island. The team was managed by John Alschuler of Hamilton, Rabinowitz and Alschuler, with Olympia and York Properties, the Brumley Company – a Charleston real-estate firm – Jaquelin Robertson and Brian Shea of Cooper Robertson & Partners, Elizabeth Plater-Zyberk of Duany/Plater-Zyberk, myself as the design implementation consultant, landscape architect Warren Byrd, Thomas & Hutton, environmental engineers, and Warren Travers, as the transportation consultant.

I remember Henry Smythe, the foundation's lawyer in Charleston, driving some of us around the Island in his ancient station wagon. The pylons for the expressway, raised so it could cross the Wando River, were already complete, but at ground level the Island was still as it was when used for hunting. Two- and three-foot-high stands of grass covered the fields and the old roads. From his knowledge of the Island and from minute differences in the height of the grass, Henry could tell exactly where the roads were and never missed a turn.

The Mark Clark Expressway, I-526, divides the Island. North of the expressway, the land was at its most attractive. The south end of Daniel Island had been slowly enlarged over the years with materials dredged from Charleston harbor and from the channels in the Cooper and Wando Rivers. Some of this land was mostly mud and still settling. Early on, it became clear that the Ports Authority of South Carolina wanted this filled land at the south end of the Island and its frontage along the Cooper River for potential future use as a container port. John Alschuler recommended not trying to fight off the Ports Authority and to incorporate the container port as part of the plan. A city of Charleston regional park in the master plan forms a buffer between the port lands and the rest of the south part of the Island. Alschuler was confident that the land the Authority acquired on Daniel Island would be too inaccessible to be developed as a container port, and he was right. The South Carolina State Ports Authority did propose a container port, Global Gateway, on its Daniel Island land in September of 1999. The development would have required building a new railway line to it from a junction in North Charleston, and would also have had a big impact on local road traffic. There was immediate opposition from communities along the proposed railway route and questions in the legislature about how the necessary port infrastructure could be financed. In June 2000, the South Carolina General Assembly voted to require the Ports Authority to obtain its approval before constructing a terminal or railroad on Daniel Island.[2] The Authority eventually decided to build their new container terminal just across the Cooper River on part of the former North Charleston naval base, where a potential railway connection already existed and there was immediate highway access. The Authority has said that its Daniel Island land is surplus. They are currently still using it for dredge spoil from the harbor.

The Highway Interchange: A critical part of the plan was the location and configuration of the highway interchange which would transform Daniel Island from a remote location to a central place in the Charleston region, 15 miles from the historic center and eight miles from the airport. There was an expressway interchange under construction just to the west on Thomas Island, but no interchange committed for Daniel Island itself.

The state had made some preliminary drawings for conventional cloverleaf expressway exits and entrances in the center of the Island, with the local north-south road serving the Island shown as crossing the highway on a bridge.

What Usually Happens: The highway cloverleaf, which Lewis Mumford once described as America's national flower, is the typical configuration for the intersection between a limited-access highway and a local road. The tight circular access ramps at highway interchanges are designed to be as compact as possible, to minimize the amount of land that must be purchased for them. These intersections often confer great value on the surrounding land because they open up the area to high-intensity urban development.

As the land around a new interchange is made much more accessible, developers are likely to approach the local government seeking a change from the current agricultural or large-lot residential zoning. The authorities, pleased at the prospect of higher property-tax revenues, are likely to rezone for intense commercial development, permitting shopping malls, hotels, and office buildings. The new regulations generally apply to the whole interchange area to show impartiality to property owners on all four sides. With so much land available, the result usually turns out to be a loose configuration of buildings, each surrounded by its own parking lot. Going from an office building in one quadrant to have lunch in the shopping mall in another quadrant would require driving there; anyone who wants to walk from one destination to another would have to dodge a lot of moving cars. The empty land contained within the access ramps for the interchange becomes the most important design feature of the new development.

An Alternative Interchange Design for Daniel Island: As all the Daniel Island land belonged to one owner, I saw an opportunity to put into practice ideas for alternatives to a conventional interchange I had presented in meetings at the Regional Plan Association and would advocate in my book, *The Fractured Metropolis*, as a way of preventing the fragmented development that typically takes place around highway interchanges.[3] We could make access from the highway an integral part of Daniel Island's town center and keep the town center a seamless part of the rest of the Island.

The Mark Clark Expressway becomes a bridge as it rises to cross the Wando River to the south-east. The main road connecting the north and south parts of the Island could go under the highway and be part of the street system for the town center. On and off ramps from the highway could connect to the main road, so that driving off the highway could lead directly to the middle of the community. This unconventional arrangement had the merit of being much cheaper to build than the usual interchange, and eventually the South Carolina Department of Transportation agreed to it, thanks in large part to the effective advocacy of our traffic consultant, Warren Travers. The actual funding of the interchange was part of an agreement that conveyed the south-west part of Daniel Island to the Ports Authority for their possible future container port. The new interchange also allowed us to plan an office park within walking distance of the downtown center. While the planning team was influenced by traditional models, we felt that an office park was a valid contemporary land use: not all the office space had to be in the town center, although it was important that it was close by.

River Landing Drive is the expressway exit and entrance for eastbound traffic. Coming off the highway, there is an immediate right turn for

Fairchild Street which is the entrance to an office park, or straight ahead to Island Park Drive and Seven Farms Drive, the main streets of the town center, which both connect under the highway to the on and off ramp for westbound traffic which is kept close to the highway and is not a location for development, as shown in this aerial view from 2022 when development was nearing completion (7.1). This view along Central Island Street, part of the street system contained within the interchange, shows typical suburban buildings usually found on isolated sites but instead forming part of a walkable town center (7.2). The parking for the retail center is contained within the block. This view shows an exit from the retail parking on to Seven Farms Drive, a main road on the Island that is also part of the interchange (7.3).

The Natural Setting and Rising Seas: Much of the perimeter of Daniel Island is marshland and our plan was to leave the marshes untouched. As it is all under the jurisdiction of the South Carolina Coastal Council, we would have had difficulty changing it in any case, but we saw the marshland as a positive frame for the development we would propose. Many of the trees on the Island had been flattened by Hurricane Hugo a few years before, but the remaining trees, particularly parallel rows which had been planted to lead up to houses which had once existed on the Island, were incorporated in the plan wherever possible. We were aware of the possibility of sea-level rise. The plan was laid out to keep the developed part of the Island above sea level after a rise of three feet, which at the time was not expected until the end of the 21st century.

Managing storm and flood waters using the marshes as a natural drainage systems was also part of the master plan concept. The Charleston office of Thomas & Hutton recommended sizing the storm drains at larger diameters than the minimum required and designed the drainage system to have holding areas that then empty through the marshes, filtering the water before it runs into the Cooper or Wando Rivers. There is also a 20-foot buffer area between all development and the edge of the marshes. Daniel Island has come through all major storms so far without serious flooding damage to roads and buildings.[4] A direct hit from a hurricane as strong as Hugo in 1989 would undoubtedly cause more severe damage, and rising sea levels will gradually drown the protective marshes. At some point in the future, the Island will need flood walls to replace the marshes.

A Plan Based on Neighborhoods: We planned residential development on the Island as a series of walkable neighborhoods connecting to a trail system that leads into the many acres of preserved land and parks. The actual configuration of the streets, parks, and lots was designed by Brian Shea of Cooper Robertson. North of the highway was always seen as the most valuable land and was planned with a country club and golf courses as its central element, surrounded by walkable neighborhoods with their own parks and trails. There are a great many golf courses and golf-course communities in the area; and

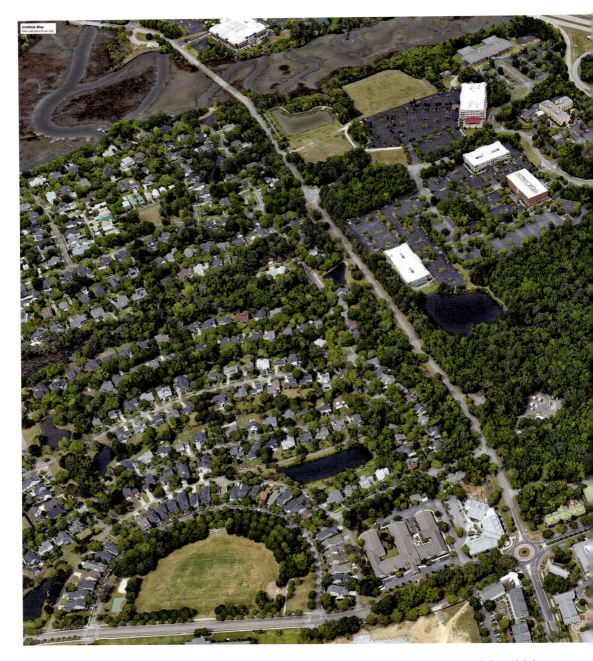

7.1 An aerial view of the central part of Daniel Island shows the highway interchange at right, with its access ramps integrated with the streets of the town center and not forming the usual tight circles of a highway cloverleaf. The first two residential neighborhoods can be seen at left.

Within the town center, buildings are organized along the streets, and, in addition to shops, there are offices and an apartment complex. At ground level, the parking is landscaped, but its extent is revealed when seen from the air. It may be that, in the future, if more people work from home and fewer people come into the office every day, some of the land occupied by parking could become available for more office buildings, or for other uses.

The residential complex within the town center, and another one just to the south-west have their parking contained within multi-story garages, but the smaller apartment buildings near the waterfront south and west of the town center have at-grade parking, its extent again revealed in the aerial, although well landscaped and hidden within the blocks at ground level. The main streets near the interchange are wide, but in the residential neighborhoods visible on the left side of the aerial it has been possible to make the tree-lined streets narrower.

Daniel Island is a big improvement over most suburban development, but it is still car-centric, an inescapable part of suburban life today.

7.2 A street within the Daniel Island Town Center leads to office buildings and an apartment complex. The area is walkable, but the streets are still required to be wide enough to accommodate suburban rush-hour traffic. It is possible that, in the future, part of the space occupied by such wide streets can be repurposed for stormwater management.

7.3 A one-way exit street from the landscaped parking area of the Daniel Island Town Center retail district. The landscaped parking is contained within the blocks, and it is possible to park once and walk to several destinations. Visible in this view is a lake located between parking areas within the town center, which reduces the amount of parking visible at one time, but development is still spread out by the demands of parking.

it was clear that what was offered at Daniel Island had to be special. The Daniel Island Club is Charleston's only 36-hole golf-course complex, with championship level courses designed by Tom Fazio and Rees Jones. Daniel Island and especially North Daniel Island turn out to have a national market as a second home and retirement community, which was anticipated in the original plan, but was not considered a certainty.

Implementing the Plan: While the master plan was being approved by the city of Charleston, Matthew Sloan, who had been working with John Alschuler managing the planning process, moved to Charleston as the project manager for the foundation. In 1997, after the plan was approved and construction had begun, the foundation sold the property to the Daniel Island Company. Matt Sloan became the chief operating officer and one of the owners along with Frank W. Brumley. Investors in Daniel Island developments have included Crow Holdings (the holding company of the Trammell Crow Family), Greystar Capital Partners, and J. Ronald Terwilliger (then the chairman of Trammell Crow Residential).

Designing the First Neighborhoods: The first two neighborhoods were developed before the highway interchange was completed at a location which was accessible from local streets and the Thomas Island interchange. Brian Shea's original plan was redesigned in more detail, with occasional paths between the houses, so people could walk to the edge of the marshes. A community recreation center was placed between the two neighborhoods where it could be reached on foot as well as by car. There was a small city park in one neighborhood, and a larger, semi-circular park as the focal point of the other neighborhood. They are on the left in the aerial view, 7.1.

But everyone who lives on Daniel Island still needs to have access to a car. The master plan called for neighborhoods where garages are either reached from alleys, or, if the garages face the street, are set back at least 25 feet behind the front facade of the house to keep sidewalks as uninterrupted by driveways as possible. Organizing houses around walkable streets was new in the suburban Charleston market at the time, and was still unfamiliar in most parts of the United States. Today, rules like this are expected, at least in new urbanist developments, but then there were no available stock plans for builders that fit the garage requirements or the kinds of narrow, deep lots we were laying out at Daniel Island. Matt Sloan commissioned a series of stock plans, which met the guidelines and fit the lots, from an experienced plan service; and these plans were included in the first set of architectural and landscape design guidelines for builders. I wrote the first set of architectural guidelines. I avoided overt historical details, but suggested elements and proportions drawn from traditional South Carolina residential buildings, which was also more or less what most developers were already building. If developers wanted to use a historic detail, the guidelines promoted authenticity, such as a requirement that window shutters be operable and cover the window opening when they were closed. Some builders initially complained about the extra hardware costs, but they had the alternative of not using exterior shutters at all. Today, operable shutters are considered a selling point for houses on the Island. Houses in the first neighborhoods go at resale for more than triple their initial cost.

Town and Community Centers: South of the Highway, Seven Farms Drive was planned as both a main street of the town center and the location for institutional uses. Bishop England High School had outgrown its old site in central Charleston and the Daniel Island Company donated a site for them opposite the semi-circular park in the second neighborhood. The high school was one of the early developments on the Island and its presence proved to be a significant attraction for home buyers, with people moving to the Island anticipating that their children would attend the high school. The Berkeley County School District has built a K-8 school, in the south end of the Island, within comfortable walking distance of many neighborhoods and next to the Charleston public library branch. There is a recreation center at Governor's Park, both just north of the town center, built and operated by the city of Charleston. There is also a private Early Childcare Center for children of ages 1–4, the Daniel Island Academy.

The Daniel Island Company also worked hard to make commercial buildings in the downtown at least two stories high, which was important if the buildings were going to be in proportion to the streets and blocks – which had to be wide because they were effectively part of the highway interchange. The market was accustomed to single-user commercial buildings one-story high on individual properties, and it took patience and ingenuity to put tenants and developers together to make the two-story buildings possible. The Daniel Island Company's own office space started off on the second floor over a bank. Matt Sloan says: "Today we have the opposite problem; we have to keep telling people the height limit is four stories." The interchange which brings people to the Daniel Island downtown from around the region and the presence of the office park have helped a true downtown retail center grow up, with specialty shops and a diverse choice of restaurants, as well as local convenience stores.

The architectural guidelines for the town center require buildings to "hold the street wall," that is be constructed along a build-to line laid out close to the sidewalk. There is a gas station in the downtown, but the pumps are in the interior of the block, behind the associated convenience store which is up at the sidewalks on the corner. The supermarket and its parking lot are also mid-block, next to the elevated highway, so the parking lot does not face a main street. Charleston landscape architecture firm Design Works and architect Chris Schmitt are among the professional firms in the region who have worked with Matt Sloan to solve detailed design and planning problems as implementation continued.

Daniel Island now has some 7,500 residential units, including four-story apartment buildings in the town center where there is also some affordable housing. A million square feet of office space has been built on the Island, including cellular telephone company SunCom, a health insurance company office, and the headquarters of the National Golf Course Owners. Another tech firm, Blackbaud, moved its offices to a larger building in the town center. Their original building, along with a soccer stadium Blackbaud had sponsored next door, have now been demolished to make way for apartments. A remaining regional destination is the Family Circle Tennis Center on the waterfront across from the downtown district.[5]

Implementation strategies

Could the Daniel Island highway interchange become a prototype? Integrating the interchange with the development that is likely to grow up around t requires planning before the highway is open and in use, while the engineering drawings for the highway and its interchanges are still being prepared. There could be planning grants to the jurisdictions around each proposed new interchange through the state agency building the highway. The local governments could then prepare master plans to centralize walkable, mixed-use, intense development within one quadrant of the interchange where it would be readily accessible from all four directions and could become a mixed-use walkable center. Other land close to the interchange could develop as houses and apartments, not downtown uses. The master plan, discussed and approved by the community, would then be the basis for zoning changes when it was time to make these decisions.

On Daniel Island, it clearly helps that the streets that connect the east- and westbound parts of the interchange can pass under the highway structure at ground level because the highway had to be elevated to cross the Wando River. It also helps that all the land around the interchange belongs to the Daniel Island Development Company, ably run by Matthew Sloan to create permanent value, not just a quick profit. Having an innovative developer certainly made it easier to build an innovative street plan.

In another situation, achieving a comparable result would be possible by elevating the highway just long enough to clear the local connecting road. It is even possible, although less desirable, for the connecting road to go over or under the highway. The key is designing entrances and exits to feed right into an urban street system and not just be confined to circles as close as possible to the highway right of way.

A comparable street network to the one on Daniel Island could be mapped and built by a local government, implementing a plan arrived at by a public process. With advance planning, all the land around an interchange can be made part of a special zoning district, or the landowners could form a development corporation for their shared properties, with the design approved as a planned unit development. The long-term advantages of a highway interchange that fits seamlessly into the real estate it generates have been clearly demonstrated at Daniel Island.

Designing for future sea-level rise was part of the Daniel Island plan from the beginning, although looking back 30 years later, the scientific projections at the time were probably too optimistic. So far, however, the Island has remained safe from storms that could have flooded a more conventional development.

Offices, apartments – including some affordable units – and a retail center are integral parts of the community. They may be typical suburban buildings, but they are part of a completely different development context of connected streets and parks. The residential neighborhoods at Daniel Island are all walkable and are closely related to parks and open space. Schools, libraries, and recreation are close by. The Island's large size and single ownership helps make this innovative development possible, and it has benefited from the support by the city of Charleston. However, the equivalent of Daniel Island is being built in suburbs all the time, but made up of tracts of single-family houses, shopping strips, and isolated pockets of offices or other commercial development. The same investments could be redirected toward a much better-designed result.

8

USING BUS RAPID TRANSIT IN SUBURBS

Is there any way to make suburban development in the United States less car-dependent? Maybe. Bus Rapid Transit can be feasible in some suburban situations, especially along highways which have been zoned for commercial development. Bus Rapid Transit is a new way of using buses to emulate rail rapid transit. It can run on existing roads and highways and does not need expensive supporting structures. Conventional light rail services, which are proven to generate development within walking distance of stations along their route, have high capital costs because foundations for rail transit always require excavation, especially when foundations must go below the frost line wherever freezing temperatures are possible. Suburban highways which might become transit routes cover distances which are too long and have population densities too low to make any kind of rail transit financially feasible.

Bus Rapid Transit: A relatively inexpensive rapid transit system using buses running on ordinary streets and highways was first deployed at a large scale in Curitiba, Brazil beginning in 1974.[1] These buses operate in the same configurations as light rail. There is a dedicated bus lane, comparable to the space occupied by rail tracks. The stops are weather-protected and spaced at intervals comparable to station stops on transit lines. There are articulated multi-section buses creating capacities comparable to the vehicles in a rail system, and passengers board and leave through multiple doors, having bought their tickets before, just like for rail transit.

The Health Line, a true Bus Rapid Transit line, comparable to one in Curitiba, runs along Euclid Avenue between downtown Cleveland and the uptown University Circle District. It was estimated to have generated $9.5 billion of new investment within half a mile of the line, including both construction and other economic benefits, along the Euclid Avenue corridor at the time of the line's 10th anniversary in 2018. The 9.4-mile-long line cost $200 million to build.[2]

This map of the line in 2008 (8.1) shows that its middle section had many areas of vacant land, a pattern similar to development in many suburban commercial corridors hard hit by on-line shopping and the COVID-19 pandemic. This central part of the Health Line runs through

DOI: 10.4324/9781003384106-9

USING BUS RAPID TRANSIT IN SUBURBS

USING BUS RAPID TRANSIT IN SUBURBS

8.1 This map shows the route of the Health Line, a Bus Rapid Transit line completed in Cleveland in 2008. It runs from downtown Cleveland, at left, to the uptown University Circle Area at right. The development along the middle part of the route appears similar to what is found along suburban commercial corridors, a high ratio of parking lot to buildings. Areas around the station stops can benefit from improved access and become more densely developed. The drawing is by Sasaki, the planners and landscape architects for the route.

one of Cleveland's most disadvantaged areas. The real-estate market in most suburbs ought to be stronger.

So far in the United States, Bus Rapid Transit in suburban areas has operated on dedicated busways repurposed from disused railway rights of way, or along HOV lanes on highways. These services offer faster trips but do not do much to change development along the route. Some communities claim to already have Bus Rapid Transit on ordinary streets, but if there is no dedicated bus lane, there are frequent stops close together, and passengers file past the driver to show or buy their ticket; the transit is not going to be rapid enough to be the equivalent of light rail.

The Case for Transit-Based Development in Suburbs: Peter Calthorpe, one of the founders of the Congress for the New Urbanism, has been a strong advocate for the environmental preservation necessary if the constructed environment is to remain sustainable. He put together transit and environmental preservation to propose that all new suburban development should be concentrated within walkable places located around transit stations. Peter prepared a plan for the Thousand Friends of Oregon, completed in 1992, which demonstrated that projected growth of the Portland metro region could be accommodated in walkable communities centered around transit stops. The houses would be closer together than in typical suburbia but not as dense as development in most Portland neighborhoods. This plan helped win an argument to stop the development of a proposed new highway and replace it by funding for new rail transit lines.

Peter's friend, Douglas Kelbaugh, when he was the chair of the department of architecture at the University of Washington, organized a workshop where visiting architects, working with teams of students, developed designs for what Doug called "Pedestrian Pockets," published in 1989 as the *Pedestrian Pocket Book, A New Suburban Design Strategy*.[3] Peter's contribution was an early formulation of his ideas about organizing walkable places in suburbia around transit, which he had been developing in architecture studios at the University of California, Berkeley, and in his planning practice. Peter published a map of how transit could create a new structure for suburban development in his 1993 book, *The Next American Metropolis, Ecology, Community, and the American Dream.* He used a fan-shaped, half-circle to map a new residential neighborhood, with the opposite side of the circle either omitted to deal with existing conditions or reserved for commerce and industry. The landscape apart from these places should be developed to much lower densities or not developed at all[4] (8.2). This proposal has not received enough attention because people assumed that it wasn't possible to build conventional transit on routes like these. Bus Rapid Transit, with its far lower capital costs, could be a way of making this kind of development pattern possible.

USING BUS RAPID TRANSIT IN SUBURBS

8.2 This graphic, from Peter Calthorpe's 1993 book, *The Next American Metropolis*, maps light rail and feeder bus lines as a way to structure growth in suburban areas around station stops, leaving much of the remaining countryside unurbanized. Light rail has not proved to be feasible in places with such long distances and so little existing development. However, Bus Rapid Transit could be effective in this kind of situation, and there are prototypes for driverless feeder bus lines which might have low-enough operating costs to also be feasible.

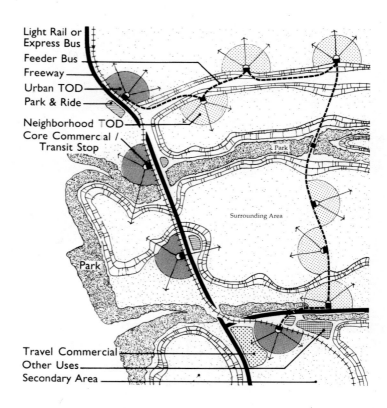

Peter Calthorpe's semi-circular diagram is based on the five- and ten-minute walking patterns observed in older communities with legacy rail transit systems. The area of greatest transit use is within a five-minute walk of the entrance to a transit station. There is a diminishing area of additional influence extending to a ten-minute walk to or from access to transit. It is well documented that more intensive development takes place within walking distance of rail transit stops.

Ordinary bus transit does not seem to create the same kinds of development opportunities as rail transit. In most places, buses are too slow, too infrequent, and the routes are too easily changed for developers to make investment decisions based on buses. But the stations on newer rail transit systems, notably in the Washington, D.C., and San Francisco metro areas, are now generating more intensive development, helped along by favorable zoning policies and sometimes by redeveloping parking sites owned by the transit authorities. Many other metros with recently constructed light rail or streetcar lines are also seeking to create transit-oriented development (TOD) around the stops, notably in the Minneapolis and Dallas metro areas.

The Case for Walkable Destinations: Research into walking patterns in developed areas shows similar patterns to research about walking to and from transit stops. People are very willing to walk for five minutes, which at a walking speed of three miles per hour means a quarter of a mile, or about 1,300 feet. If there is a good reason to make the trip, and the walk is interesting, most people are willing to walk for ten minutes, thus covering half a mile, about 2,600 feet. These numbers have had a big influence on the design of shopping malls, determining the distances between anchor stores and the overall length of the whole complex.

Walkable distances were also behind the well-known diagram of the neighborhood unit, put forward by Clarence Perry in an article published in 1929.[5] His neighborhood map shows a five-minute walk from the center to the periphery and a ten-minute walk across the neighborhood from one edge to the other (8.3). Perry was arguing for the continued building of walkable neighborhoods, which at the time were already under threat from new patterns of development being created by automobiles.

Perry's diagram was adapted by Andrés Duany and Elizabeth Plater-Zyberk in the 1980s for what they call traditional neighborhoods and the concept became a key element of their influential urban design practice (8.4). Their work has demonstrated that walkable neighborhoods are a popular real-estate concept. While many people like suburbia just the way it is, as much as 40 percent of the housing market can be attracted to the successful walkable neighborhoods the Duany Plater-Zyberk office has designed for many developers across the United States and in other countries.[6]

Andrés and Elizabeth were also among the founders of the Congress for the New Urbanism in 1993, which has been an effective advocate for traditional neighborhood design and for TODs.

Commercial Corridors Are Becoming Land Banks: The familiar suburban commercial corridor, a highway lined on both sides by strip shopping centers, restaurant franchises, motels, gas stations, and small office buildings, now has many vacant buildings, because of the retailing and workplace revolutions created by e-commerce and working from home, accelerated by the COVID-19 pandemic. These corridors were already very inefficiently developed. So much land was zoned for commercial uses that it encouraged separate buildings for each enterprise no matter how small. The narrow zones left no space to create a center where different kinds of uses could reinforce each other, and people could walk from one to the other. The result has been that substantial parts of these commercial corridors have become land banks. There will never be enough of their original uses to fill them up again.

The Urban Land Institute, a non-profit research organization supported by the real-estate industry, has been looking to improve

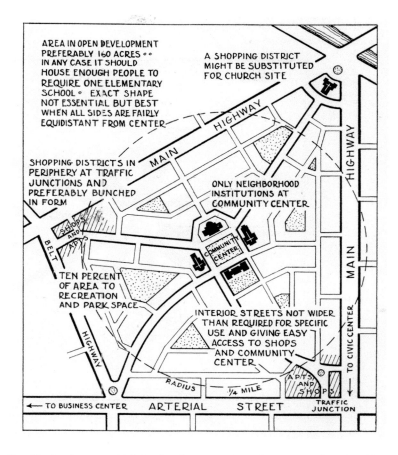

8.3 If suburban growth is to develop around station stops, what should it look like? This well-known and influential diagram by Clarence Perry of a walkable suburban neighborhood is from his essay in the 1929 *Regional Plan for New York City and Its Environs*. Perry based his proposal on the assumption that the outer edge of a neighborhood should be no more than a five-minute walk from the center, and that it should be possible to walk across the whole neighborhood in ten minutes. The population, according to Perry, should be dense enough to support a neighborhood elementary school – which leaves unanswered the question of how big the school should be. It is interesting that Perry, even in 1929, did not expect suburban neighborhoods to be supported by transit. The most likely place for a transit stop would be in the lower right-hand corner of the diagram where it could serve three other neighborhoods as well. The five-minute walk radius would be drawn centered on the transit stop. Most of each neighborhood would be within a ten-minute walk.

suburban commercial corridors for a long time. Back in 2000, I participated in a day-long discussion at the ULI offices about suburban commercial strips, which were already widely understood to be over-supplied with retail space broken up into uneconomic units. The comments from this meeting were assembled into a publication which made ten recommendations, including "pulsing" commercial

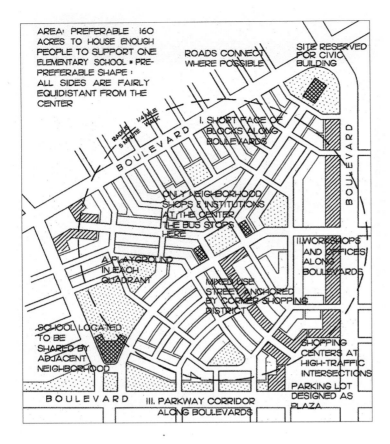

8.4 Andrés Duany and Elizabeth Plater-Zyberk revised Perry's diagram to meet more recent conditions. They show the elementary school at the neighborhood periphery to be shared with other neighborhoods, reflecting the reality that elementary schools today are generally larger than they were in 1929. They assume bus service and note that the bus stops in the center of the neighborhood. That would be local service, however. The center is not a good place for a BRT stop as the streets leading to it are not shown as wide enough to have exclusive bus lanes. The BRT stop should be at the junction of four neighborhoods.

development to concentrate it in strategic locations.[7] I also participated in a ULI study of an evolving commercial corridor in Prince George's County, just outside Washington, D.C. which came to similar conclusions. The ULI has continued to publish studies about reimagining commercial strip development, defining it as a public health issue.

Another set of recommendations for reinventing suburban commercial corridors, which recognized that far too much land was zoned for retail and office, was published by the U.S. Environmental

8.5 Development along a suburban commercial highway corridor could evolve so that the most important commercial uses take place at major intersections, as described in this diagram.

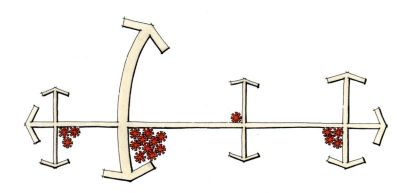

Protection Agency in 2010. It included designs for by the firm of Freedman Tung + Sasaki which described concentrating the remaining commercial development at busy intersections (8.5) and changing from commercial to multi-family zoning in the places in between[8] (8.6). n our book, *Reinventing Development Regulations*,

8.6 In between the concentrated commercial development, the land could be rezoned to permit apartments and town houses. This drawing and the previous one are by Freedman Tung + Sasaki for a report by the U.S. Environmental Protection Agency in 2010.

Brian Blaesser and I recommended making this kind of development possible by amending most commercial zones to permit apartments and row houses, and reducing, or even eliminating, parking requirements for stores and offices, based on studies that show that local regulations typically require far more parking than is actually needed. Developers would be free to build as much parking as they thought necessary but would not be compelled to reach a specific ratio.[9]

Both "pulsing" development as the Urban Land Institute recommended and concentrating commercial uses at key intersections as recommended by the U.S. Environmental Protection Agency could be reinforced by a transit system that would support walkable places. True Bus Rapid Transit, with frequent service, dedicated lanes, well-spaced transit stations, multiple doors, and fare cards which can be purchased before boarding can support walkable neighborhoods and walkable business centers at an affordable cost. The operating costs are not so different from any other bus line, and the infrastructure to support it does not add that much to the normal cost of a street or highway. The additional investment in Bus Rapid Transit can pay off by supporting more compact development that reduces growth pressures on the urban fringe, which always require extensive supporting investments in roads and infrastructure.

Designing the Health Line: I happened to be part of the team doing the initial planning for what is now Cleveland's Health Line. The team was directed by Hunter Morrison, then Cleveland's planning director, and Craig Amundsen, a vice president of engineering firm BRW.[10]

The problem with running transit on Euclid Avenue is that it is just under 100 feet wide. That space has to accommodate sidewalks, transit lines in both directions, platforms at the transit stops, and still leave room for automobile traffic. There were basically two design options. The transit could run next to the sidewalks, or in the middle of the street. If the transit lines ran next to the sidewalks in both directions, passengers could wait for the transit on the sidewalks, and there would be more room on the street for auto traffic. However, rail transit lines next to the curb meant no stopping by other vehicles and no deliveries, and there were serious traffic problems making turns at intersections or at mid-block entrances to parking. Transit in the middle of the street meant building transit stops there, accessed from crosswalks at intersections. Part of the street space needed for the stops could be created by narrowing the sidewalk where the stations occurred, creating curving traffic lanes. There was not enough room for two lanes of traffic in each direction, and the final light rail plan showed only one lane for cars and trucks on each side of Euclid, and no parking.

8.7 This aerial view from Google shows the dedicated Bus Rapid Transit lines at the center of Cleveland's Euclid Avenue. The stations are also in the center of the right of way, reached by crosswalks at the intersection. The eastbound station stop is on the upper left of this view, the westbound at lower right.

Although our study of the line on Euclid Avenue was for light rail transit, Cleveland's Regional Transit Authority decided to replace the light rail with exclusive bus lanes for a true Bus Rapid Transit system. Sasaki was the planner for the BRT line on Euclid Avenue, which opened in 2008. The bus lanes are located in the middle of the street, in a configuration very similar to one we had studied for light rail. The transit is a tight fit, because Euclid Avenue is much narrower than a typical suburban highway. The aerial view along the completed project, 8.7, shows how the bus lanes, traffic lanes, turn lanes, and station stops are configured in the final design. The bus stops are on islands between the traffic lanes and the bus lanes and are reached by crosswalks at the intersections (8.8). The transit vehicle currently in use, with its multiple doors for both entry and exit, is shown in 3.9.

An important factor in the success of this line is that it connects two significant destinations, while running through lower density areas in between. As most suburban commercial corridors grew up along streets much wider than Euclid Avenue, they could accommodate dedicated bus lanes and transit stops much more easily. There are many suburban places where a Bus Rapid Transit line could help restructure development along its route while connecting two established centers. Cleveland's Health Line is an example, already implemented, which shows what could be possible.

8.8 This view, also from Google, shows one of the weather-protected station stops.

Implementation strategies

The key strategy is broadening the travel options in suburbs to include transit that people are willing to use because it is frequent, goes close to where they wish to go, and is both comfortable and affordable. The most important advantage of building Bus Rapid Transit to fill this need is its much lower initial cost compared to any transit system which requires rails. As most communities already run bus services, they have an operating agency which can manage the upgraded transit. Yes, the more frequent service needed to attract riders means more buses and more drivers, but that investment can pay off over time in increased property

8.9 The vehicle currently being used on the Health Line. Longer Bus Rapid Transit vehicles are available, if demand on the line should require them.

USING BUS RAPID TRANSIT IN SUBURBS

valuations around the transit stops, and more mobility for employees and customers.

Placing Bus Rapid Transit stops along commercial corridors, supported by development regulations that permit mixed uses, could facilitate the transition to new, more profitable uses for many distressed suburban properties. Retail which requires people to actually show up, like restaurants, health clubs, or hairdressers, can cluster in the locations served by transit. Apartments and row houses, which are often scarce in suburbs, can fill the land between the transit stops and still be within walking distance of the transit. People in the neighborhoods on both sides of the transit stops will also be able to walk to both shops and transit.

9
MOBILIZING SUPPORT TO REDESIGN AN ENTIRE CITY

Cities are being built, and rebuilt, all the time by different types of private real-estate companies, by local governments and school boards, by public works departments, by highway engineers, by transit agencies. Large amounts of money go into changing cities every day. Usually, these investments achieve far less than they could. Urban design can give some coherence to uncoordinated actions that are happening anyway, and, in Omaha, Nebraska, I had an opportunity to help bring more design direction to what was already being invested in their city.

In 2002, I was finishing up my work with HDR on the Destination Midtown plan for Omaha discussed in Chapter 4. I was in Omaha for a Midtown meeting, and Douglas Bisson from HDR came to breakfast with me at my hotel along with Connie Spellman from Lively Omaha, an organization founded the year before by three Omaha business leaders: Bruce Lauritzen, the head of the major local bank, John Gottschalk, the CEO and publisher of the Omaha World Herald, and Ken Stinson, the chairman of the Kiewit Corporation, an Omaha construction company with projects across the country. The Lively Omaha program had grown out of the Chamber of Commerce and Connie Spellman had moved over from the staff of the Chamber to run it, with the objective of making the city more competitive in attracting and keeping people and businesses. They wanted an urban designer to take Omaha through a process that would lead to more planning and development decisions being informed by design. Doug Bisson was the leader of community planning and urban design at HDR, but HDR was involved in too many local projects to take the lead role in a plan for Lively Omaha. Would I have any ideas about how I would do this?

I said that creating a constituency for urban design across the whole city would require a community involvement process looking at issues step by step, which would probably take a whole year. There would also need to be an advisory committee which should include representatives of all the interests that would have to agree to changes: community leaders, business executives, construction-union leaders, real-estate developers and their lawyers, design and planning professionals, and government officials – including at least one City Council

DOI: 10.4324/9781003384106-10

member and someone from the mayor's office, as well as leadership from the city's planning and law departments. To chair the public meetings and the advisory committee, Lively Omaha would need to identify a highly respected individual who was also perceived as fair and neutral and persuade that person to take on this role. I needed to think about how to coordinate these two processes, but there were several ways to do it.

I had recently become a consulting principal at WRT, a planning and design firm in Philadelphia, and had access to the people I needed to help me do what Lively Omaha was looking for, but there was at least one additional consultant I wanted to involve. I also needed to sit down and figure out what this would all cost, but I would get a proposal back to Connie Spellman as quickly as I could. Connie said that this was exactly what they hoped I would do; however, while she could raise the money, provided the proposal looked reasonable, the funders would insist that they understand the full financial commitment up front. They didn't want to be faced with requests for additional money in the middle of the process.

My first move was to call Brian Blaesser at the Robinson and Cole law firm. We had worked well together on the plan for Wildwood, Missouri, and respected each other's opinions. I explained the Omaha situation and said I needed him for advice to make sure the design and planning concepts we propose could be translated into official plans and regulations. I would also need him to be present at meetings so he could explain the legal context and answer questions. Designers have very little credibility with anyone who finances real estate; and government officials are usually convinced that they already know the law, and what they are doing now is the only possible alternative. I added that there would almost certainly be a second phase to the work rewriting zoning and other regulations. At that point, Brian's firm should take the lead, and I would become an advisor to provide continuity. Brian said he would be interested, but we both needed to know what kind of time commitment we were talking about.

I worked out a year-long process for studying alternatives, arriving at agreed on design concepts with both community leaders and the public, and identifying means of implementation. I reviewed the schedule and cost estimates with my WRT colleagues, and with Brian, and our proposal was accepted in Omaha, with the understanding there would be a separate implementation phase, which Brian would lead, which would include any necessary revisions to existing regulations.

A group of leading businesses and foundations funded the process through the Omaha Community Foundation. Mayor Mike Fahey became an enthusiastic supporter, contributing the participation of the planning department and other city agencies. Del Weber, the former chancellor of the University of Nebraska Omaha, became the community leader who would preside over the process. He and Robert Peters, the planning director, were named co-chairs, but Bob asked Del to run the meetings. Connie Spellman worked with the city to create a review committee representing all the categories of people who would have to agree if the city were to adopt major changes in the way it managed development. Over the course of the study, she also arranged for speakers to carry the message to community and business groups, and she went to many meetings herself with the funders backing the project, and with business and political leaders, to make progress reports and explain the urban design process. Her staff managed the logistics of the review committee and public meetings and organized and distributed all the public information. She changed the name of the process from "The Omaha Comprehensive Urban Design Plan," which had been the title of my proposal, to *Omaha by Design*. "As opposed to *Omaha by Default*," said Bob Peters. Soon Connie would change the name of her organization from Lively Omaha to Omaha by Design.

In my proposal, I had divided the issues into three subsets – Green, Civic, and Neighborhood – which correspond to three potential constituencies for urban design: environmentalists, organizations of civic, business, or cultural leaders, and neighborhood activists, including representatives from the city's most disadvantaged communities. Relating development to the city's hilly terrain, designing desirable and recognizable places, and creating equitable conditions across all communities would be basic issues within the Green, Civic, and Neighborhood categories.

We realized that if we opened the review committee meetings to the press and the public, the committee members would be less likely to speak frankly. Our solution was to have a presentation and discussion with the review committee at lunch, followed by a public meeting that evening with the same presentation, often improved by comments made at the earlier review. Some committee members attended the public meetings so they could hear and report on what was said. The Omaha World Herald and the TV channels covered the public meetings, and the World Herald ran articles about the Green, Civic, and Neighborhood issues beforehand, which helped produce a large turnout, never less than several hundred people.

I made all the presentations to both the review committee and the public meetings. Nando Micale was the project manager at WRT, overseeing the graphic production and making some of the drawings himself. Brian Blaesser came to Omaha for every presentation, answering questions in meetings and adding supportive comments. With his cell phone, he was also able to keep up with a lot of his other work during these trips.

I made it a principle that my WRT colleagues and I would not propose anything in Omaha that had not been implemented successfully somewhere. What would be special in Omaha would be applying urban design comprehensively to a whole city. We also decided to work within the framework of Omaha's recently completed master plan. This permitted us to concentrate on design, and not unlock all the interrelated variables about issues such as infrastructure, health-services, and education. All the master plan components have design implications, but revisiting every recently made decision would have stopped us before we got started.

Green Omaha: Omaha has a hilly topography, with creeks running along the valleys. Many of these creeks now run at the bottom of deep constructed channels, and what people saw from the trails that run along them are the backs of buildings, dumpsters, and service entrances. The buildings along the creeks make it impossible to restore the meandering streams and wetlands that were once there. But the waters of Brush Creek in Kansas City had been raised by breakaway dams, a design concept I had included as part of the Plaza Urban Design and Development Plan described in Chapter 5. The result is a stream that looks like a river, rather than a trickle at the bottom of a concrete culvert. Here was a successfully implemented design that could be a mode for Omaha. Our slides of Brush Creek and our drawings showing Omaha's creek waters raised and the banks landscaped helped convince people that creek frontages could be assets.

Omaha is subject to sudden heavy rainstorms and flash floods. Public safety issues should keep development out of the flood plains along the creeks. We showed how flood-protection policies in Tulsa, which has a similar weather pattern and ecology, have had the effect of creating a citywide open-space system along the creeks there. So our proposal was to combine necessary flood protection with the landscaped creeks to form a park system that adds value to the whole city, especially to the properties outside the floodplain but facing the creek.

New Federal water-quality standards and flood protection both require retaining stormwater on the hillsides flanking the creeks. We showed examples and made drawings of green parking lots, a direction suggested by a participant in one of our community meetings, to show how water retention could be achieved by landscaping within the parking lot, rather than detention basins, saving land area for the developer. Landscaped parking fields could also reduce the heat-island effect from large areas of uninterrupted paving. Comparable concepts have been implemented in other communities by modifying requirements for parking and water retention which are already in subdivision ordinances.

Omaha's turn-of-the-last century park and boulevard plan created scenic drives along the ridge lines and a legacy of green streets in the older parts of Omaha. The 1,800 acres of sparsely planted land on the fringes of Omaha's limited access highways could also be opportunities for large-scale landscape design. We showed highway landscaping in California and in cities like Charlotte and Chicago, and made drawings to demonstrate how trees, native grasses, and flowering plants could make big changes in the experience of the highway at costs within the means of corporate sponsors or private donors.

The city already has programs for planting and replacing street trees, but the subdivision ordinance did not require developers to plant trees on new residential streets. Since tree planting requirements

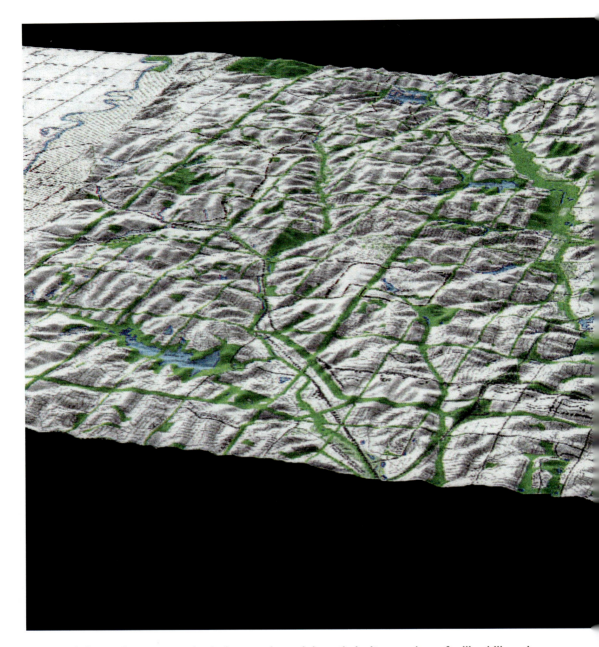

9.1 People in Omaha were surprised when we showed them their city as a place of rolling hills and valleys; they were not used to thinking about the city that way. The streams that run through the valleys, the city's parks and boulevards, and a new program of encouraging tree planting along a network of green streets could produce a connected green setting for Omaha's neighborhoods and business centers.

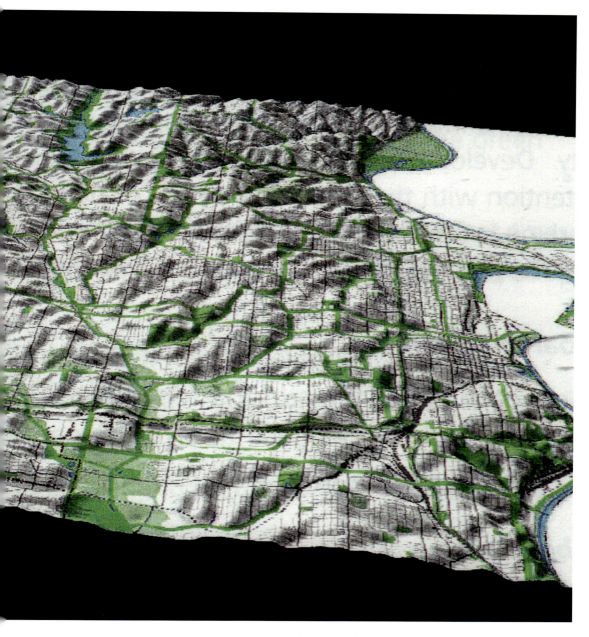

are routine in subdivision ordinances, we suggested adding them in Omaha. We also delineated a network of "green streets," where tree planting and landscaping would be most important.

We showed how these proposals could lead to a connected system of tree-lined streets, parks, waterways, and landscapes that would become the setting for Omaha's neighborhoods and business centers (9.1).

Rapid urbanization of the city's surrounding farmland was another prominent Green issue. The city has already reserved future suburban park sites in its master plan, since its planning jurisdiction extends three miles from its current borders. The master plan also designates areas where population densities should be kept low to preserve environmentally sensitive areas. We would have liked to have proposed growth boundaries to reinforce these provisions. The population of Omaha had been growing at the rate of 1 percent a year, but land was urbanizing much faster than would be required by population increases alone, as is true almost everywhere in the United States. Growth boundaries had been considered for the master plan, but not included, since Nebraska law does not support the kinds of growth boundaries that are in force in Oregon. However, policies we proposed under the Civic heading can result in greater residential and office densities within already developed parts of Omaha. Attracting some development away from the edges can slow down the rate at which farms give way to urbanization. The city can also decide how much land is urbanized through its annexation policies, which we addressed as part of our discussion of civic design.

Civic Omaha: We asked the review committee to help us list the most memorable places within the city, the places that received the most use, and the gathering places for public events. The results confirmed our observation that Omaha's Dodge Street is comparable to Atlanta's Peachtree Street or Los Angeles's Wilshire Boulevard, linking a series of important locations extending westward from the original downtown. Most of the other important places are along major north-south streets that connect to Dodge.

It would be confusing to call all these areas downtowns, so we called them "areas of civic importance," but together they function as the downtown of the metropolitan city Omaha has become (9.2). We proposed that these areas of civic importance be mapped in the zoning ordinance as overlay districts. The areas within each overlay should be subject to the kinds of design guidelines for building placement, pedestrian access, and concealing service areas used in successful downtowns elsewhere. Urban designers have had extensive experience in managing downtown development and can point to many successful outcomes. Government investment in streets and other public spaces is just as important as the standards placed on private development. We proposed new commitments for planting street trees, providing high-quality streetlights, and rationalizing traffic and parking information signs within the areas of civic importance. The design guidelines for private investment we proposed were principally about the relationship of buildings to streets, just as they are in traditional downtowns, but allowing for the differences in scale.

It will take a long time to bring all the areas designated as civically important up to a downtown standard, but it has to begin in order to happen at all. In addition to legislation and public investment, it will require the creation of business improvement districts to mobilize the resources of the stakeholders within each sub-area. Just as owners have not thought of their land along Omaha's creeks as waterfront property, the property owners in these areas of civic importance have

9.2 We asked our Working Review Committee members to identify the places in Omaha they felt were most significant for everyone and were most used by the community. These places turned out to be along Dodge Street, the main connecting street running westward from the city center, and on a few north-south streets that crossed Dodge. The result was this map, drawn by Yan Wang at WRT, a satellite view of Omaha at night showing what we called the Places of Civic Importance.

not thought of themselves as having the opportunities and responsibilities that go with being in a downtown.

We made designs for six Civic Place Districts within the areas of civic importance — two in the traditional downtown and four at strategic locations along the Dodge Street corridor. One of these is in Midtown Omaha, where Mutual of Omaha had already committed to a major redevelopment effort but had not yet completed their designs. We made a diagram which included their existing office building, the additional land they owned which was mostly used for parking, and the adjacent public park, using a vocabulary of build-to lines, placements for parking garages, potential building placements, plus our suggestion for integrating the park space with their land, and asterisks indicating the termination of vistas which should have special treatment (9.3). Mutual's

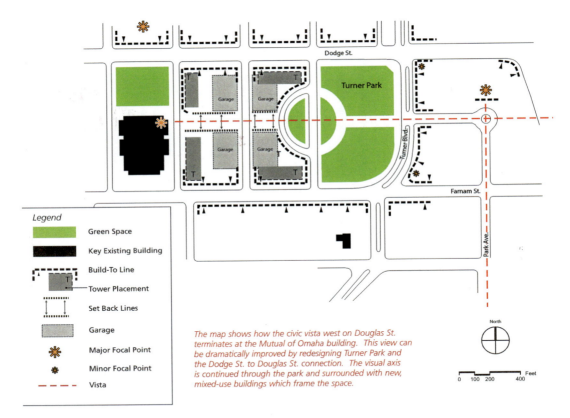

The map shows how the civic vista west on Douglas St. terminates at the Mutual of Omaha building. This view can be dramatically improved by redesigning Turner Park and the Dodge St. to Douglas St. connection. The visual axis is continued through the park and surrounded with new, mixed-use buildings which frame the space.

9.3 Example of the guidelines for a zoning overlay, a Civic Place District, for the most important locations within the Places of Civic Importance we had identified. This one is for the Midtown area where Mutual of Omaha had already committed to a major redevelopment effort, shown in Chapter 4, but had not yet completed their designs. We made a diagram which included their existing office building, the additional land they owned, which was mostly used for parking, and the adjacent public park, using a vocabulary of build-to lines, placements for parking garages, potential building placements, our suggestion for integrating the park space with their land, and asterisks indicating the termination of vistas which should have special treatment. You can compare this diagram with the actual design shown in 4.6 and other illustrations in Chapter 4.

buildings, designed by Cope Linder Architects, take up many of the ideas in the diagram but then develop them into a fully integrated design, as described in Chapter 4.

There should be more, but these special districts offer prototypes. Each is designed around one or more public places, and the design guidelines are based on the increased value that proximity to such a space can create. The feasibility of the guideline comes from the public investment, plus a substantial increase in permitted development under zoning. These are locations that have the potential to become urban places, with a mix of apartments and offices as well as retail, and that can help draw people back from increasingly remote suburban districts. Specific plans like these can create opportunities for developments not possible today because no individual property owner is in a position to organize them.

We also proposed setback/build-to lines for buildings along major commercial corridors outside the areas of civic importance, plus minimum landscaping requirements for each development, and requirements for confining above-ground utilities to one side of the street, preferably in an easement behind the buildings.

Design Standards for Annexation: Under state of Nebraska law, property owners can create a Sanitary and Improvement District in non-urban areas before they are annexed to a city. These "SIDS" can make capital improvements, supported by tax assessments within the district. When the district is annexed, the city takes over the debt obligation. Omaha can set standards for Sanitary and Improvement Districts that are ultimately expected to be annexed, by saying what will be acceptable and what will not. Omaha's master plan already set requirements for different sizes of commercial centers, from ten to 160 acres, which will be acceptable when they are annexed to the city.

We saw that this power allowed Omaha to ask for mixed-use, walkable centers instead of strip malls. We took a typical real-estate industry model, the "life-style retail center," where stores and restaurants are organized along a street, and not just facing a parking lot, and proposed adding apartments and offices to produce places friendly to pedestrians where stores, offices, and residences would all be permitted. We prepared design guidelines for these pedestrian-oriented, mixed-use centers to supplement the categories of commercial centers already in the master plan (9.4). The guidelines show street and sidewalk configurations and building placements for each category of center. These designs set up a framework that allows development to become more intense as time goes on, without rebuilding the initial structures. Such places can reach a high enough population density and include enough destinations to enable them to be served by bus rapid transit, which, in turn, will reinforce compact, walkable patterns of development and draw businesses and residents that might otherwise

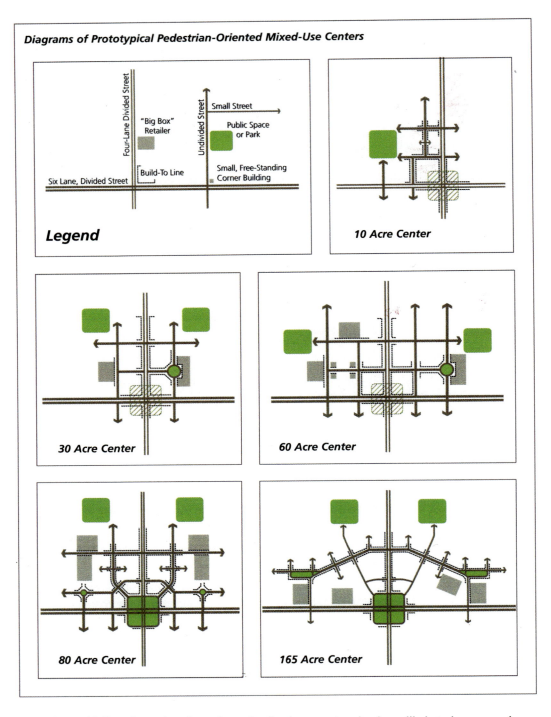

9.4 Design guidelines for pedestrian-oriented, mixed-use centers in places likely to be annexed around the periphery of Omaha supplement the requirements for the categories of commercial centers already in Omaha's master plan. Following these standards can be required if the developers of a new district in a rural area want it to be annexed by the city.

go even farther out. We made drawings to show how this transformation could take place at key locations.

Our other civic design proposals set standards for illuminating significant buildings and other structures, like highway bridges, and call for more funding for public art, and for the establishment of a design review board to advise on the interpretation of design guidelines and control the quality of publicly financed projects.

Neighborhood Omaha: Omaha has many separate areas considered to be neighborhoods; more than 70 neighborhood associations maintain websites and issue newsletters. There are too many of these organizations for the city to respond to each effectively. Our Midtown study had helped create an alliance of neighborhoods, where leaders got to know each other by participating in the planning process. We proposed that the city draw boundaries that would create 14 Neighborhood Alliance Districts, not unlike Washington's Advisory Neighborhood Commission Districts, New York City's Community Planning Districts, and planning districts in other cities. Mayor Mike Fahey immediately saw the value in doing this and made it his policy before we had even finished our plan. We proposed that each of these Neighborhood Alliance areas should receive help from the city in developing its own plan, as I had observed was the policy in Norfolk, Virginia. These plans would take the Green and Civic principles established citywide and applying them at a smaller scale. The Neighborhood Alliance plans should also deal with preserving and enhancing retail in older neighborhoods and adding neighborhood retail and other amenities in post-1950 neighborhoods. We provided illustrations showing how such plans could be done.

We also illustrated how to create walkable neighborhoods with their own retail and civic centers as the city expands. New traditional neighborhoods are sometimes created as part of individual developments; we showed in Omaha how neighborhoods where people can walk to some destinations could become the usual way development in new areas takes place. Four neighborhood units as defined by Clarence Perry and adapted by Andrés Duany and Elizabeth Plater Zyberk fit into 640 acres, the area contained within a square which is one mile on each side. Much of the United States has been laid out with a grid of major streets intersecting at every mile. Omaha, like many other U.S. cities, grows by annexation and a mile-square grid surrounds the city on three sides. The city has a park plan which identifies land that should be set aside as parks or as nature preserves in areas that may be annexed by the city. As part of the Omaha by Design plan, we suggested that Omaha also make walkable neighborhood units part of the SID standards, which are mandatory for land that the city is expected to annex. We prepared a diagram showing how that could work (9.5). The squares at the intersections of the major streets could be retail centers serving the four adjacent neighborhood units (9.6).

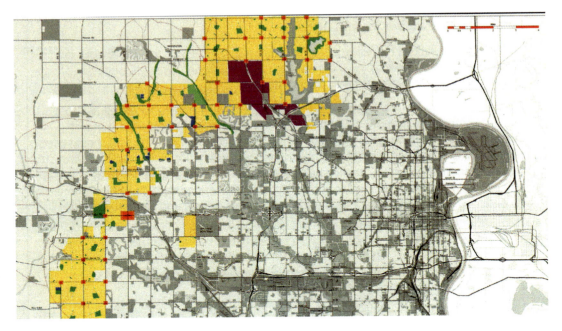

9.5 Omaha's Parks Master Plan had already identified land that should be set aside as parks or as nature preserves in areas that may be annexed by the city. As part of the Omaha by Design plan, we suggested that Omaha also make walkable neighborhood units, as described in the previous chapter, part of the SID standards, which are mandatory for land that the city is expected to annex. We prepared a diagram showing how that could work. The result would be compact, walkable neighborhoods and commercial centers that could be served by bus rapid transit. There would be less demand to urbanize additional land, and a better design for the land that would be urbanized.

A school could be located at these intersections as well. All the neighborhood units would relate to one of these centers. Instead of a series of sprawling residential subdivisions, walkable neighborhoods — and walkable commercial and civic centers — could become the usual way development takes place. These compact communities could eventually support a bus rapid transit system, as discussed in the previous chapter.

Omaha by Design gave everyone in each community meeting three cards: green, yellow, and red — like traffic lights. After I explained a proposal from the podium, I would ask people to hold up the card that best suited their reaction. Often, I would see green cards across the auditorium, but sometimes there would be a lot of yellow, or even red: obvious signals that we needed more discussion, or a revised proposal.

Implementation Strategies: Brian Blaesser advised us from the beginning that we had to have a consensus about what we wanted to accomplish before we got into extended discussions about how to write new regulations. As the planning process neared completion, planning director Bob Peters suggested that the first step toward implementation should be the adoption of our work as the official Urban

MOBILIZING SUPPORT TO REDESIGN AN ENTIRE CITY

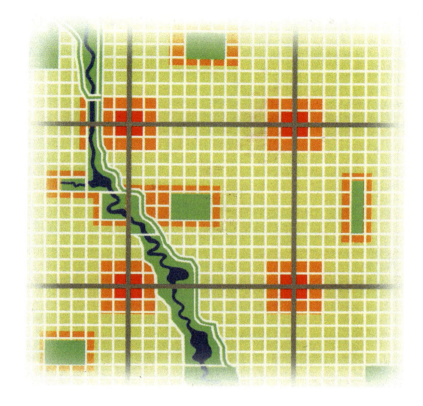

9.6 This diagram is a close-up of the design concept shown in 9.5. The red squares are commercial centers, the orange areas are apartments or town houses located close to commercial centers or parks, yellow shows locations for individual houses, all parts of walkable neighborhoods.

Design Element of the Master Plan, something actually called for in Omaha's Charter. Such an element had never been prepared and was not included when the city adopted its latest Master Plan. Our final report became the draft Urban Design Master Plan Element, along with a framework report by Blaesser setting forth the legal basis for future implementation measures. Altogether, the 21 Green, Civic, and Neighborhood goals, objectives, and policies require 73 implementation proposals, including administrative changes by the city, legislative changes, capital projects, and opportunities for privately funded initiatives. The last of the public meetings in the Omaha by Design process endorsed these proposals.

The Omaha World Herald printed a 16-page insert for the Sunday newspaper that gave a much bigger audience an opportunity to examine the text and illustrations of the urban design goals and rank them from high priority (1) to lowest priority (5), either by sending back a form that was part of the insert or by answering the same questions on the Omaha by Design website. More than 1,300 responses were received. As the survey was available on the web, a few responses came in from outside the city, including one from Vancouver and several from Texas. All 21 goals received strong support; the score for most goals averaged in the high 1s or low 2s; very few people checked 4 or 5. The objectives receiving the most support are those that produce the most benefit for the most people: green streets, the park system along the creeks, high quality of public buildings, conservation of older buildings, preservation of older neighborhoods, and guidelines for creating neighborhoods in new areas. The Civic Place Districts and other goals requiring guidelines for building design also scored well, but not as well. Public art, lighting landmarks, green parking lots, and highway beautification, which I had expected would be urban design measures everyone would support, struck respondents as less of a priority.

The Urban Design Element was approved unanimously by both the Planning Commission and the City Council and is an official part of Omaha's Master Plan.[1] The changes to the ordinances implementing the Urban Design Element, which were developed in a second phase of our study, led by Robinson & Cole, with design diagrams by WRT, are included in ARTICLE XXII – URBAN DESIGN in the Omaha zoning ordinance. It can also be read on-line.[2] Omaha also now has an Urban Design Review Board, as we recommended.

Connie Spellman continued as the executive director of Omaha by Design until 2015 and built it into a powerful advocacy organization for urban design, which it continues to be.[3]

Community participation has become a standard practice in making all planning and urban design decisions. But getting real engagement from everyone likely to be affected is still challenging. Our Omaha effort did well using the technology available at the time, but newer on-line resources could have widened participation even more. And the community has to see results. Nothing is more alienating than bringing a whole community to a consensus and then having the urban design plan officially turned down and never implemented. That is why our advisory committee in Omaha was so important. We did not bring anything to a public meeting without knowing that our advisors would support it, which sometimes meant several iterations with the advisors before a proposal came to the community.

Communities are better at saying what they don't like than inventing design proposals, although our focus on green parking lots in the Omaha plan came from a suggestion made during a community meeting. Most of the time the design professionals have to set the agenda, but arriving at a consensus about design is very different from devising a complete design in advance and expecting everyone to like it. And of course, even when consensus is reached, there will still be some people who don't agree. But they will know that their red cards are a small minority, and they will probably understand why many of their neighbors voted the other way.

10

DESIGNING FOR REGIONS AND MEGAREGIONS

Cities are becoming multi-centered regions and these regions are growing together to form megaregions. This trend was already discernable in the 1950s when urban geographer Jean Gottmann wrote about what is now called the Northeast Megaregion in a book published in 1961 in which Gottman called development from Washington to Boston a *Megalopolis*.[1] Describing the number and configuration of megaregions that have grown up since Gottmann's research has produced a variety of different maps. One recent book identifies 13 megaregions in the United States after an extensive analysis of national trends:

- Northeast – from the Hampton Roads, Virginia metro area north through Washington, New York, and Boston up to central Maine
- Piedmont-Atlantic – from the Birmingham, Alabama metro area through Atlanta, and then north through Charlotte and Raleigh, North Carolina
- Florida – including most of the Florida peninsula from the Miami metro region northeast through Jacksonville, and also west along the I–4 corridor to Tampa and other west-coast Florida cities
- Midwest – extending in several different directions from Chicago north and west to Minneapolis, through Michigan and Ohio as far east as Pittsburgh and Rochester, and south to St. Louis, and, along a different corridor, to Lexington, Kentucky
- Central Plains – north from the Oklahoma City metro area through the Tulsa region to Wichita and Kansas City
- Texas Triangle – a corridor running from the San Antonio region north through Austin to Fort Worth and Dallas and connected at both ends to Houston
- Houston is also part of the Gulf Coast megaregion, extending from Brownsville and Corpus Christi through New Orleans to Mobile, Alabama
- Front Range – from Albuquerque north to Colorado Springs, Denver, and Fort Collins
- Basin and Range – from the Salt Lake City metro region north and west to Boise
- Arizona Sun Corridor – from the Phoenix metro area south to Tucson and north to Flagstaff

DOI: 10.4324/9781003384106-11

- Southern California – from San Diego/Tijuana through the Los Angeles metro region to Santa Barbara, also including Las Vegas, Nevada on the other side of the mountains
- Northern California – the Bay Area and south through the Central Valley to Fresno and north to Sacramento, also including Reno, Nevada
- Cascadia – from Eugene, Oregon north through Portland, Olympia, Tacoma, Seattle and on to Vancouver, British Columbia[2]

Florida, the California megaregions, and Cascadia exhibit the kind of continuous growth that characterizes the Northeast megaregion, but there are some big stretches of open land between metropolitan areas in many of the other regions. The Basin and Range megaregion is more of a set of relationships among relatively small, separate metros, rather than an example of continuous urbanization. The Midwest and Piedmont Atlantic megaregions have both stretches of continuous development and large stretches of rural land. However, all the megaregions are predicted to absorb a high proportion of the population growth expected by midcentury; and places that are discontinuous now can be expected to become more closely connected.

A big proportion of the new development in these megaregions has taken place, and continues to go forward, without any meaningful design direction. Growth has followed the interstate highway system, energized by the high profits that can be realized from urbanizing farms and woodlands when they are made accessible by new highway interchanges. Local development regulations continue to be based on the century-old zoning and subdivision ordinances which remain blind to the natural environment. Commercial zoning continues to be mapped in narrow strips along local highways, too much land zoned for commerce to be used efficiently, and not enough in any one place to permit the development of walkable centers. Residential neighborhoods continue to be rigidly segregated by lot size, which in many places means segregation by income, and little ability to walk to destinations. The rush to new development opportunities has led to the hollowing out of many older areas, even within growing megaregions. This pattern is often referred to as suburban sprawl, but, as discussed earlier, it is not an accident. It is the default result of government actions intended for other purposes without considering their effect on the design of the communities that result. The real-estate industry has adapted to the opportunities this default system provides to the point that other options can no longer seem possible. People who like their suburban lifestyle are not aware that it could be better, and that it does not have to come at the expense of other people who have lower incomes or whose mobility is restricted by age or disease.

Development Choices for the Seven-County Orlando Region: Megaregion development in Florida has been driven by tourism and a very rapid growth in population, attracted by the climate – warm in the winter and moderated by air-conditioning in the summer – by low taxes, and by aggressive recruitment of business from other parts of the country. Continuing urbanization in Florida is altering the natural environment, endangering water supplies, displacing agriculture, and compromising the attractions which bring so many visitors and permanent new arrivals.

Linda Chapin, Director of the Metropolitan Center for Regional Studies at the University of Central Florida and former chair of the Orange County Commissioners, had become concerned about what development trends were doing to her part of Florida. In 2005, she asked me to organize a research project at the University of Pennsylvania to design a plan that would look forward to 2050 for the seven-county region around Orlando.[3] The study would be staffed by advanced city planning students who were in their last semester before receiving their graduate degrees. This was an opportunity to look at the set of problems which affect the growth of entire megaregions.

The methodology I intended to use was comparable to what I had used for Arden Heights in New York City and for the Village of Irvington: show existing conditions, project what would happen if current development trends continued, and then show a better alternative that would be feasible within current development practices. We were not working for the state of Florida or any other governmental authority, but Linda intended to use our study as the basis for public meetings throughout the region, building a constituency for a better future.

Fortunately, tools were available that would allow us to take our method of showing a trend and an alternative up the scale of a seven-county region. Andrew Dobshinsky, one of the researchers, whose previous degree was in digital media design, introduced me and the other participants to ESRI's ArcGIS and its Spatial Analyst Extension.

Using Geographic Information Systems (GIS) allowed us to understand how to depict growth in the Orlando region at a far greater level of detail than would be possible by conventional mapping techniques based on aerial photos and U.S. geological survey maps, and our predictions would be more precise than if we simply drew possibilities by hand.

Andrew showed us how to input criteria into the computer program that would show, decade by decade, where the predicted people would be likely to locate. The computer program used a version of the gravity models familiar from transportation planning. The likelihood of population locating in a particular place was determined by the relative attractions that the place offered. Putting the attraction values into the computer program required judgment calls that assigned values to such factors as proximity to jobs, proximity to already developed areas, receptivity of zoning to new development, accessibility to transit or to highway interchanges, availability of unbuilt land, and so on. The computer program could make land that was already dedicated for conservation inaccessible to projected new development.

The first step was a trend model. What would population distribution look like if future development followed current trends? Florida already had population projections up to 2030 by county from the state's Bureau of Economic and Business Research. To bring the numbers from 2030 up to 2050, we averaged four different methods of projecting the population growth.

To determine future trends, the study used attraction values based on current development patterns. Once these inputs had been determined, the computer program would show the population patterns derived from all these inter-related variables. The result showed a decade-by-decade advance of low-density development across the landscape. The computer map also gave us a way to input the location of environmentally sensitive land, and the trend model gave a picture of how much of the five regional ecological systems the study had identified was likely to be urbanized. It was not a comfortable future. The trend model showed extensive damage to the local environment and inefficient urban sprawl that would probably become economically unsustainable before its full predicted extent could be realized.

We went to Orlando and visited each of the seven counties. Linda had organized people to show us around and brief us on local issues. We also attended meetings set up to give us a sense of current economic trends and development prospects.

We were then in a position to design an alternative to the trend.

Florida, like most other parts of the country, relies on cars for almost all personal transportation, except in Miami, which has a local rail transit system and a downtown automated people-mover, similar to the systems that link terminals at some airports. In the seven-county Orlando region, the only alternatives to travel by car at the time were buses, but their services were slow and infrequent.

Florida had been studying a high-speed rail system to link Miami to Tampa through Orlando, with a later extension up the east coast to Jacksonville. It had been authorized by a constitutional amendment in 2000, but repealed by the voters in 2004, the year before our study.

We decided that Florida had been right the first time, and that we should reinstate the high-speed rail line as part of the alternative to the trend that we would prepare. At station stops on the high-speed line within our study area, we postulated that there would be local transit systems, perhaps rail transit as in Miami, but possibly bus rapid transit in smaller urban areas.

Florida also already had a state program for acquiring environmentally sensitive land and taking it out of the real-estate market. We decided that Florida should use this existing program to invest in acquiring environmentally sensitive land that would otherwise be in the path of development trends.

DESIGNING FOR REGIONS AND MEGAREGIONS

In our study, we then mapped transit systems that could develop decade by decade up to 2050, assuming that the high-speed rail line connecting Miami to Tampa through Orlando would again become state policy. The study also identified critical station stops and designed local transit systems to link up with them, thus identifying places where more intense development would be most likely because of new transportation access.

Our study continued to use the map of the most important environmentally sensitive land, which we had seen being over-run by development in the trend model, postulating that in the alternative, all the environmentally critical land otherwise threatened by the development trend could be preserved by being purchased by a Florida government program.

New attraction values based on higher densities made possible by the high-speed rail line and the transit systems were fed into the computer program, based on what could be constructed during each decade based on the population projections. The effect on the environment was assessed after a trial run of the computer program. Land that should be preserved and was shown to be threatened with urbanization was made inaccessible in the computer program, which was then re-run. The resulting computer map, with environmentally sensitive land protected, then became the basis for mapping the next decade of population growth and deciding which additional land needed to be preserved.

The study tabulated the differences between the trend and the alternative, decade by decade. The overall message from the study was clear. The alternative model produced by our iterative process could be compared, decade by decade with what could be expected to happen otherwise. The two 2050 maps summarize the study (10.1 and 10.2).[4]

Linda Chapin reprinted our report in a much larger edition with a cover letter describing it as a wake-up call for the community. The report would become the basis for a series of community meetings across the seven counties to talk about the choices they would need to make in the years ahead.

Two years later, Linda Chapin asked me to prepare another study using a similar methodology but this time for the entire state of Florida, to be funded by the 1,000 Friends of Florida.

I asked Andrew Dobshinsky, now a graduate, to be the co-director of the study, he ping the participants input criteria into the computer program that would show, decade by decade, where the predicted population would be likely to locate. The 1,000 Friends had already commissioned a trend model from the GeoPlan Center at the University of Florida. It had population projections for 2020, 2040, and 2060, and it used GIS to map how the effects of the projected population growth would spread over the landscape. We heard

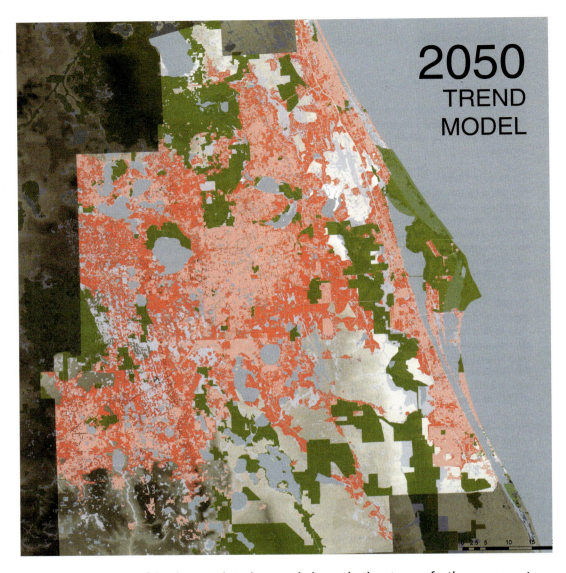

10.1 A GIS-based map of development based on population projections to 2050 for the seven-county Orlando region. The program allocates the development according to a model based on extrapolation of current development trends.

10.2 An alternative GIS-based map of a better development pattern for the seven-county Orlando region by 2050. The computer program included preserving environmentally sensitive land that would otherwise be threatened by the development trend and adding transit as an attractor for higher-density development that would take some of the pressure off development at the urban fringe. The transit assumption produces the higher-density corridors, shown in a darker red, radiating out from the center of Orlando to significant destinations in the metropolitan region.

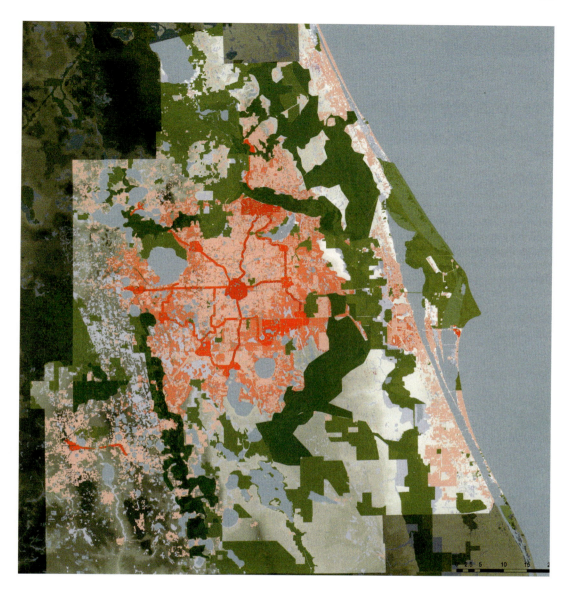

informally that their work had been influenced by the methodology of our 2005 study, widely circulated by Linda Chapin. The GeoPlan trend, like our previous study, did not assume any additional land conservation purchases, but they did use future highway plans from the Florida Department of Transportation in mapping their trend, while assuming that all additional transportation improvements would be for highways or airports. They did not include the effect on coastal areas from sea-level rise. They accepted that urbanization of rural land would be inevitable and should be facilitated by approvals, and by building the necessary infrastructure, including new roads and highways. They assumed that average current development density in each county would remain the same in the future, and that new development would remain much the same as it had been, without additional environmental protections.

The trend computer model gave us details of how development could play out across the state and was an effective standard of comparison for any alternative we would propose.

The participants in our study this time devised a more sophisticated method of describing which parts of the rural environment needed to be conserved than had been used in 2005. Available reports and studies were used to make maps of the highest priority lands to maintain habitats, the highest priority lands for maintaining the aquifers, the highest priorities for preserving wetlands, the most significant agricultural areas, and what was defined as "contiguity" with existing land that had already been preserved for development. Then, using the ArcGIS Spatial Analyst computer program, these five separate overlays of the map of Florida were synthesized to identify the places which most met these five sets of criteria. Determining what was defined as the ideal conservation network this way took a lot of computing power, which turned out not to be available to us from our university. Instead, the participants linked eight of their laptops, which ran the program for 14 hours to produce the map of the highest priority conservation lands combined with the land already conserved. Several people kept watch overnight to make sure that program continued to run (10.3).

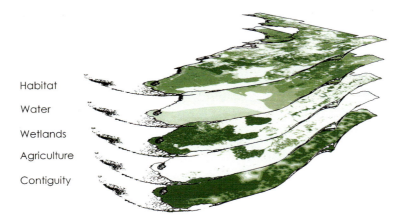

10.3 University of Pennsylvania researchers mapped five levels of environmental sensitivity in Florida shown in these stacked maps. From the top: natural habitats needed to conserve diversity of species, location of water resources, including aquifers susceptible to contamination, wetlands, prime agricultural lands, and places needed to maintain contiguity – for example, species corridors to link habitats. The five maps were then synthesized to highlight the places with a high level of concurrence of these five criteria. The result, the ideal conservation network, including land areas already preserved, was one of the guides for producing the alternative to the state-wide development trend in Florida.

We then convened a week-long workshop at the University of Central Florida's downtown Orlando center. I had invited the leadership from several Florida planning and design offices to participate in the workshop, which they had agreed to do pro bono: Barbara Faga and Ellen Heath from EDAW, Tim Jackson of Glatting Jackson, Victor Dover and James Dougherty from Dover Kohl, Gerald Marston from WRT, James Moore from HDR, and Elizabeth Plater-Zyberk, then the dean of the School of Architecture at the University of Miami, along with some of her students from their urban design program.

The first day of the meeting began with a presentation of the trend model and its effect on the ideal conservation network.

I then had the whole group brainstorm the principles that should inform our work as we developed the alternative to the trend. I sat at a computer open in PowerPoint and wrote and projected the text of each principle on a screen as people suggested the wording. Everyone could see the principles as they were drafted and redrafted. We ended up with seven:

1. Protect Florida's Essential Land
2. Invest in Balanced Transportation
3. Plan for Climate Change
4. Don't Waste Land
5. Design with Nature
6. Encourage Compact Development
7. Rebuild to Create Great Places

During the rest of the week, teams from our study worked with the Florida professionals to identify prototypes of development at different densities, and they also developed several urban design plans as examples of how development should take place at higher densities in critical locations.

When we reconvened in Philadelphia, the study developed the seven principles in detail, organizing the report around them. The study included postulating the design for a state-wide high-speed rail network, plus transit systems for the principal cities, each with cost estimates. These designs provided attractors for population distribution in the alternative computer map. The study also mapped the coastal areas subject to flooding using the estimates of sea-level rise that were the scientific consensus at the time and made them off-limits to new development. We estimated acquisition costs for protecting the parts of the ideal conservation network which would be threatened by development, and when the expenditures would be necessary. We also showed how to conserve water and electric power to keep the impact of the new population down to a level similar to then current consumption. The objective, not wasting land, meant higher densities where there would be improved access. It also meant that new development should be designed to reduce negative impacts on the environment by making development more compact than the trend, saving the conservation lands, and not regrading or filling wetlands. The report used the designs produced during the Florida work session to illustrate desirable development and also used examples from around the country which had also been identified at our Florida meeting. The conclusion of the report included comparisons of estimated costs and acreages for the trend and the alternative organized by decade.

Linda Chapin came up to Philadelphia to see how we were doing and suggested that we should divide the state-wide maps of the alternative to the trend into geographic sectors so that people in Florida would be able to see what was being proposed for their region at a larger scale. This was easy to do, as the information was already on the computer maps.

Linda underwrote printing additional copies of the study[5] which were shipped to her in Florida so she could distribute them, and she also had a copy of the PowerPoint presentation. The maps showed the trend and then the much more compact development and greater environmental preservation would be possible if the policies in the alternative were followed (10.4 and 10.5). The report clearly stated that the alternative would save a great deal of public money compared to the public expenditures that would be needed because of the trend. In later years, I found that our report was often known to planners and decision-makers in Florida.

Designs for the Tampa/Orlando Super Region: In 2010, I was invited to make a third Florida study by a coalition of two business groups representing the Orlando and Tampa regions, which were working together as a super region. At the time, a high-speed rail connection from Orlando to Tampa had been funded by the Obama administration. Preliminary work had been done by the state for such a route before the high-speed rail amendment had been repealed in 2004. This work had made it "shovel ready" for funding as part of the national response after the 2008 economic crisis. It would be the first phase of the original planned line that would ultimately go on to Miami. Governor Charlie Crist, then a Republican,[6] had pursued the funding, including seeking and receiving the legislature's approval to finance and build SunRail, a local commuter train in the Orlando region which was to connect with the high-speed inter-city rail line and was considered a critical part of Florida's application for Federal funds. The Federal government had then awarded Florida 2.4 billion dollars toward building a high-speed rail line between downtown Tampa and the Orlando airport.

The two business groups urged us to present our recommendations in the context of enabling enhanced global competitiveness for the region, which we did. The money which would be spent to develop these two regions if the current trends continued could be spent more constructively to reduce wasteful sprawl and unnecessary damage to the environment. As many of our global competitors are pursuing such constructive policies, doing the same would make the United States more of an equal player.

We used the trend model based on population projections to 2060 developed at the University of Florida as we had in 2007, and also modeled preserving the rural lands across both regions, drawing on work done in previous studies. The plans for high-speed rail gave us a specific focus, allowing the participants in our study to postulate areas of higher density around the station locations, and to design regional transit for both the Tampa and Orlando areas, incorporating the construction of the SunRail stations in Orlando already committed. Our trip to Florida was divided between Tampa and Orlando, providing briefing sessions about the two regions and also allowing us to visit the planned sites for the high-speed rail stations and the Orlando transit stops. These plans made the model of the alternative to the trend much more convincing, as it appeared at the time that they were based on real-world possibilities. Again, we mapped how environmentally sensitive land could be protected and showed areas affected by sea-level rise where new development should not take place. We made a second trip to Florida to present our proposals and there was a lot of interest. The plan presented then is available on a website maintained by the World Economic Forum.[7]

In 2011, newly elected governor, Rick Scott, also a Republican, refused to accept the Federal funds for high-speed rail, to the dismay of business leaders in Florida who were strong advocates for the project. More recently, a privately funded conventional-rail connection, called the Brightline, has been developed between Miami and the Orlando airport, with an extension planned to go on to Tampa. The SunRail transit has also gone forward. With both completed, something like the conditions postulated in our 2010 report will have become a reality, and perhaps public policies for environmental and development decisions can be informed by the potentials for compact development and environmental preservation which we had identified.

A changing climate means changing plans for development in much of Florida

In 2010, the scientific consensus was still that the most significant effects of sea-level rise would not be felt in Florida until near the end of this century. We did show what was predicted, but it was not decisive. The previous prediction has now been radically revised. Recent storms have demonstrated that there are already substantial risks to Florida's coastal areas from the storm surges that accompany hurricanes, and the potential for damage will increase substantially by midcentury because of greenhouse gases already in the atmosphere, regardless of global progress in limiting emissions.

Our studies at the University of Pennsylvania could be a model for replanning the entire state of Florida. The category of environmental

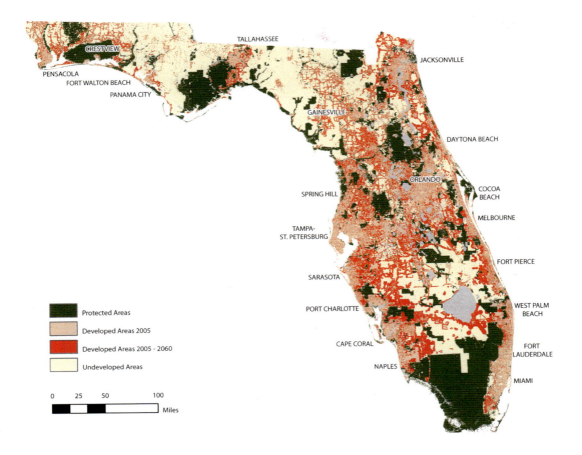

sensitivity would need to be enlarged to show areas currently, or soon to be, at risk from storm surges and even ordinary tidal flooding. They should either be off-limits to new development or given major new coastal protections. The populations who may need to be relocated from places that are no longer safe need to be added to the population growth projections, which may need to be revised downward as the risks of moving to Florida become more apparent. The trend with its inherent dangers can be contrasted with an alternative that keeps people safe, and the costs of protection and relocation can be compared with the costs of rebuilding after each new climate disaster. Climate change could be the motivation for improving how land is being developed in the Florida megaregion.

Implementation strategies

The basic urban design strategy at the regional and megaregional levels continues to be showing decision-makers and the public the difference between what will happen if current trends continue, and a better alternative which could happen if different policies are followed.

DESIGNING FOR REGIONS AND MEGAREGIONS

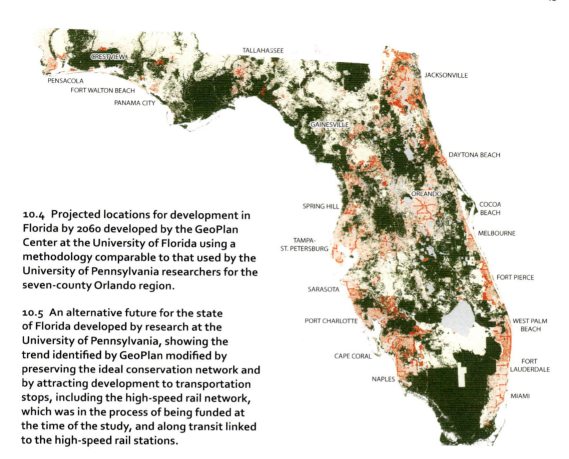

10.4 Projected locations for development in Florida by 2060 developed by the GeoPlan Center at the University of Florida using a methodology comparable to that used by the University of Pennsylvania researchers for the seven-county Orlando region.

10.5 An alternative future for the state of Florida developed by research at the University of Pennsylvania, showing the trend identified by GeoPlan modified by preserving the ideal conservation network and by attracting development to transportation stops, including the high-speed rail network, which was in the process of being funded at the time of the study, and along transit linked to the high-speed rail stations.

Creating the trend and alternative models is enabled by the latest computer-aided tools both for mapping environmentally sensitive land and for modeling projected population growth and land use according to different scenarios.

A fundamental strategy behind postulating an alternative should be a balanced transportation system that includes inter-city passenger rail connecting to airports and to local transit in cities along the route. These are both present in the Northeast Megaregion, partly as a legacy from earlier development, and they effectively demonstrate the advantages of not relying entirely on highways and airplanes for long-distance travel, and on highways alone for local travel. The passenger rail trains do not have to meet European or Asian high-speed rail standards. Equaling the Acela service in AMTRAK's Northeast Corridor for speed and frequency would be sufficient.

The other fundamental strategy is protecting the environment from people, and people from the environment, informed by the new conditions being created by a warming climate. In Florida, our studies assumed that only acquisition by the State could protect natural resources in the path of development, which seemed the only possibility at the time. Sea-level rise and its accompanying flooding dangers have changed the situation. There are now environmentally sensitive regions which are also no longer safe places to build, even with extensive re-engineering. Changes to local development regulations and new methods of managing development according to watersheds could help guide new development to safe places. Sea-level rise is putting new burdens on government, which will have to help pay for protections or pay to help people move.

The megaregions in Florida, Texas, and California are mostly within the borders of each state, which means that the states already have the power to make plans at this scale. Planning for megaregions that cross state boundaries will also have to be done by the individual states within each larger region, but there will need to be mechanisms, such as the interstate compacts which already exist for various purposes, to co-ordinate their efforts.

I have written in much more detail about ways to design megaregions in my recent book, *Designing the Megaregion, Meeting Urban Challenges at a New Scale*, published by Island Press. For more about designing for climate change, you can consult *Managing the Climate Crisis*, also published by Island Press, published in 2022, and written by me and Matthijs Bouw.

AFTERWORD: IMPLEMENTING URBAN DESIGN FOR A CHANGING WORLD

During the next decades, urban design will have a critical role in making planning and development decisions for places that will be changing rapidly. The warming climate brings with it new dangers from floods, heat, drought, wildfire, and food shortages. Essential infrastructure will need new protections. Shorelines in densely populated areas will need to be rebuilt. Many people will have to move as some places become permanently flooded, become deserts, are endangered by wildfires, or have dangerous summer temperatures. What were once established land uses will also be changing as more people work from home at least part of the time, do more of their shopping online, and participate in the sharing economy. The introduction of driverless vehicles will require changes in sidewalks, roads, and highways. The danger of global pandemics will require redesigns for both indoor and outdoor public spaces. The need to create a sustainable economy will mean designing for green infrastructure, distributed power sources, closed cooling systems, and water-saving irrigation. Advances in information technology will continue to change the way people relate to each other and to their government.

The strategies described in this book will become even more necessary as implementation of design and planning decisions become increasingly difficult, expensive, and contentious.

Public discussions about the future of shoreline areas and places close to wildlands will be critical not only at the community level but also for whole cities, regions, and megaregions. There are many parts of the United States which are in relatively little danger from a changing climate, and some of these places have been losing population. Urban design can provide a way to transform the public discussion about places that are becoming uninhabitable by considering where there may be desirable alternatives. Planning processes should include all the people who will have to make wrenching decisions about their futures. But there also needs to be a parallel process involving the officials necessary to implement any decision. There needs to be a consensus among the people involved but also among those needed to bring it about. Some alternatives may be available close to where living conditions are becoming uninhabitable, but there could also be

DOI: 10.4324/9781003384106-12

regional, megaregional, and even national designs and plans to reset-tle the people who will have to move.

Ignoring the environment and relying solely on engineering to make the land fit development plans was never a good policy, but soon it will not be an option any longer. Understanding the changing envi-ronment and preserving the protections natural systems can provide will be critical. Environmentally based development regulations will become essential, as will encouraging redevelopment of all urbanized areas into compact walkable communities, which can be kept safe effectively from floods and wildfires, and also consume less energy.

Public outdoor spaces will need to be redesigned to assume new roles as parts of green infrastructure systems for managing stormwater and, in waterfront locations, as places that can be redesigned to hold back rising seas. The dangers from global pandemics will also affect the design of indoor and outdoor public spaces as more people wish to eat or drink in outdoor restaurants whenever possible.

Streets and highways will have to be redesigned to make them safe for a mixed fleet of conventional and autonomous vehicles, and, at the same time, accommodate new green infrastructure requirements. As highways are relocated to safer locations, the way the interchanges are designed can change as well, creating an opportunity to integrate them with surrounding development.

Having objective design guidelines to manage development will con-tinue to be important both for investments in new or under-used loca-tions and for preserving historic and well-designed places.

Designing for cities, suburbs, and rural areas and finding ways to implement these designs are both becoming more challenging, but they also present great opportunities to make the physical environ-ment more stable, improve existing development, and learn from past mistakes when building new areas.

Suggestions for Additional Reading

Chapter 1, Including the Community in Design Decisions: Jane Jacobs wrote effectively about the gap between what designers and theorists thought would be good for people and what people actually want and need. Her indignation still makes *The Death and Life of Great American Cities*, published by Random House in 1961, lively reading today. But Jacobs was responding to what was happening in the 1950s before the great expansion of cities into what had once been suburbs. The most relevant part of her book today is probably the last chapter, "The Kind of Problem the City Is."

Paul Davidoff's "Advocacy and Pluralism in Planning," published in 1965 in the *Journal of the American Institute of Planners*. 31 (4) pp. 331–338, is a critique of the planning profession at the time as being overly concerned with the physical aspects of planning at the expense of understanding economic and social issues. It is also a call for community residents to have their own planner to act as their advocate when an official plan is made for their neighborhoods. Legal aid for poor defendants is offered as an analogy for how to fund these alternative plans for communities which can't afford to pay for professional assistance. What Davidoff leaves unanswered is how to resolve issues when there are conflicting plans for the same situation.

Bill Lennertz, an alumnus of the Duany Plater-Zyberk office, is the co-founder and former director of the National Charrette Institute, now at Michigan State University. He is the co-author, with Aarin Lutzenhiser, and many other contributors, of *The Charrette Handbook: The Essential Guide to Design-Based Public Involvement*, published by *Routledge*, 2nd Edition 2017. It is a step-by-step guide to how to prepare for, organize and run a planning and design workshop with a community, and how to take the resulting plan through the approval process.

Chapter 2, Protecting the Environment: The book which did the most to define the conflict between the natural environment and what gets built continues to be Ian McHarg's *Design with Nature*, originally published in 1969 and still in print in an edition published by Wiley in 1995. But McHarg was writing before climate change was understood as a major issue. An up-to-date approach is described in *Building with Nature: Creating, Implementing, and Up-scaling Nature-based Solutions*, by Erik van Eekelen and Matthijs Bouw, naio10 publishers, 2021.

For how to amend zoning ordinances to make them more related to both the natural environment and a changing climate, see Chapter 1, "Relating Development to the Natural Environment," and Chapter 2, "Managing Climate Change Locally," in *Reinventing Development Regulations* by Jonathan Barnett and Brian W. Blaesser, Lincoln Institute of Land Policy, 2017, pp. 7–73. This book can be downloaded without charge from the Lincoln Institute website.

Also see *Managing the Climate Crisis: Designing and Building for Floods, Heat, Drought, and Wildfire*, by Jonathan Barnett and Matthijs Bouw, Island Press 2020.

Chapter 3, Designing Cities without Designing Buildings: Much of the conversation about using development regulations to implement urban design has been conducted by the Congress for the New Urbanism. A good introduction is *Codifying New Urbanism, How to Reform Municipal Land Development Regulations*, published by the American Planning Association and the Congress for the New Urbanism, as Planning Advisory Service Report Number 526. This report leans heavily on the concept of Transect Zones, a way of rewriting zoning based on selected building types at a range of densities, rather than by traditional land-use categories. Converting zoning to transect categories makes everything built under the existing zoning non-conforming, which is a huge administrative problem if anyone wants to alter an existing building. The transect is also based on building types that embody New Urbanism, which are often not what the development industry normally builds.

A more generic way of incorporating design within development regulations is defined by the term *Form-Based Codes.* The design regulations I describe in this book are all form-based. However, many people use form-based as a way of describing transect categories. My own view is that it is not necessary to use the transect categories to integrate design into development regulations, and the transect terminology is actually an impediment to adopting design requirements. See Chapter 6, "Establishing Design Principles and Standards for Public Spaces and Buildings," in *Reinventing Development Regulations* by Jonathan Barnett and Brian W. Blaesser, Lincoln Institute of Land Policy, 2017, pp. 147–178.

Chapter 4, Enhancing Public Open Spaces: Jan Gehl has written several influential books about designing public spaces in a way that will make people want to use them. The most recent, and the most comprehensive, is his *Cities for People* published by Island Press in 2010. Gehl reprimands designers for seeing public space only in an aerial perspective, whereas a space is only meaningful when it is experienced at eye level. He illustrates the points he makes with many photographs and measurements.

Space and Anti Space by Steven Peterson and Barbara Littenberg, ORO Editions, 2020, is a theoretical work, illustrated by examples of their own designs, which contrasts what is required to make a successful public space with what they call anti-space, often created by modernist designs, where the open areas are what is left over after the design of streets and buildings.

Public Places, Urban Spaces: the Dimensions of Urban Design is a comprehensive text book by Matthew Carmona, Steve Tiesdell, Tim Heath, and Taner Oc. A second edition was published by Routledge in 2010.

Chapter 5, Preserving Existing Urban Designs: There is an extensive literature about preservation of historic buildings and of groups of buildings considered to make up a historic district, but there is no comparable literature, or legal and financial support, for preserving an urban design. An urban design that has been implemented over decades is often no longer perceived as a design. It is just there, taken for granted by everyone. A book that can be helpful in recognizing an underlying urban design is *The New Civic Art: Elements of Town Planning*, by Andres Duany, Elizabeth Plater-Zyberk, Robert Alminana, and other contributors, published by Rizzoli in 2003. A more detailed book about an important aspect of urban design, *Great Streets*, by Alan B. Jacobs was first published in 1993, by the MIT Press. Both books were intended to give designers the information they need to emulate the examples, but they can also function as a guide to what was originally intended for a particular urban setting.

Chapter 6, Changing Regulations to Prevent Suburban Sprawl: *Crabgrass Frontier, The Suburbanization of the United States* by Kenneth T. Jackson, published by the Oxford University Press in 1984, is an important explanation of why inequality has been built into U.S. suburban development. Its chapter 11, "Federal Subsidy and the American Dream, how Washington Changed the American Housing Market," contains significant original research about government red-lining policies. Another useful explanation of how suburbs have become what they are today is contained in Chapter 2, "The Misplacing of America," in *Changing Places, Rebuilding Community in the Age of Sprawl* by Richard Moe and Carter Wilkie, published by Henry Holt in 1997, pp. 36–74.

For amending the regulations that are perpetuating suburban sprawl, see Chapter 3 "Encouraging Walking by Mixing Land Uses and Housing Types" in *Reinventing Development Regulations* by Jonathan Barnett and Brian W. Blaesser, Lincoln Institute of Land Policy, 2017, pp. 75–104 and Chapter 1, "Relating Development to the Natural Environment," mentioned earlier.

Chapter 7, Reinventing Suburban Development: *Case Studies in Retrofitting Suburbia: Urban Design Strategies for Urgent Challenges*, by June Williamson and Ellen Dunham-Jones, Wiley 2021, follows on from an earlier publication by the same authors, *Retrofitting Suburbia: Urban Design Solutions for Redesigning Suburbs* published in 2011. The more recent book is a compilation of plans and photos for 32 completed projects in the United States, introduced by several chapters which extract strategies from the cases. The urban design strategies are not about physical design but are directed toward improving public health, supporting an aging population, and helping communities compete for jobs. The case studies are either descriptions of retrofits of existing suburban developments or new developments that replace large existing projects that had outlived their original use or design, including parks, shopping centers, and office parks. The *Sprawl Repair Manual* by Galina Tachieva, published by Island Press in 2010, is a compilation of design ideas for changing existing suburbs, derived from the practice of Duany Plater-Zyberk and Company.

Chapter 8, Using Bus Rapid Transit in Suburbs: Robert Cervero and Danielle Dai found in 2014 that there was evidence that development around BRT stations did become denser after a BRT route went into operation. Their findings were published as "BRT TOD: Leveraging transit oriented development with bus rapid transit investments" in *Transport Policy* Volume 36, November 2013, pp. 127–138. Robert Cervero, along with co-authors Hiroaki Suzuki and Kanako Luchi, prepared a report for the World Bank, *Transforming Cities with Transit: Transit and Land-Use Integration for Sustainable Urban Development*, which was published by the World Bank in 2014. They include BRT as a transit option in this study, which is about the transit-land-use connection more generally.

Chapter 9, Mobilizing Support to Redesign an Entire City: Richard Florida is a well-known advocate for changing city policies to make them more attractive to business, and to make people want to live in a city, by fostering what he calls the Creative Economy. *Who's Your City, How the Creative Economy is Making Where to Live the Most Important Decision of Your Life* is directed at people choosing among cities and summarizes earlier books by Florida which were directed at policy makers. Florida's research is controversial, but he is easy to read and makes the case that communities need to pay attention to what makes them attractive, or could make them attractive. A readable explanation of why walkable neighborhoods and business centers make economic sense both for cities and their residents – as opposed to current suburban growth patterns – is *The Option of Urbanism* by real-estate expert Christopher B. Leinberger, Island Press, 2009.

Chapter 10, Designing for Regions and Megaregions: Peter Calthorpe and Robert Fulton's *The Regional City: Planning for the End of Sprawl,* published by Island Press in 2001, contains descriptions of successful regional plans, including for the Portland, Oregon metro region and for the emerging megaregion in Utah. For the latest research on megaregions, see *Megaregions and America's Future* by Robert D. Yaro, Ming Zhang, and Frederick Steiner, Lincoln Institute of Land Policy 2022. For the framework needed to implement designs for megaregions, see *Designing the Megaregion, Meeting Urban Challenges at a New Scale* by Jonathan Barnett, Island Press 2017.

Illustration Credits

1 Including the community in design decisions

1.1 City of New York.
1.2 Imagery © 2022 Google, Imagery © 2022 Bluesky, CNES, Airbus, Maxar Technology, Sanborn, USDA, FRAC, GEO Map Data © 2022.
1.3 Imagery © 2022 Google, Imagery © 2022 Bluesky, CNES, Airbus, Maxar Technology, Sanborn, USDA, FRAC, GEO Map Data © 2022.
1.4 Imagery © 2022 Google, Imagery © 2022 Bluesky, CNES, Airbus, Maxar Technology, Map Data © 2022.
1.5 Courtesy Beasley Associates.
1.6 Drawing by Yan Wang, Courtesy WRT.

2 Protecting the environment

2.1 From a handbook of standards for planned unit development published by the New York City Planning Department.
2.2 From a handbook of standards for planned unit development published by the New York City Planning Department.
2.3 From a handbook of standards for planned unit development published by the New York City Planning Department.
2.4 Imagery © 2022 Google, © 2022 Bluesky, Maxar Technologies, USDA/FPAC/GEO Map Data © 2022.
2.5 Imagery © 2022 Google, © 2022 Bluesky, Maxar Technologies, USDA/FPAC/GEO Map Data © 2022.
2.6 Courtesy Jonathan Barnett and Steven Kent Peterson.
2.7 Courtesy Jonathan Barnett and Steven Kent Peterson.

3 Designing cities without designing buildings

3.1 New York City Department of Planning.
3.2 New York City Department of Planning.
3.3 Imagery © 2022 Google © 2022 Bluesky, CNES/Airbus, Maxar Technologies, Sanborn, USDA/FPAC/GEO Map data © 2022.
3.4 Image capture May 2022 © Google.
3.5 Imagery © 2022 Google Imagery © 2022 Maxar technologies, Sanborn, U.S. Geological Survey, USDA/FPAC GEO Map data © 2022 Google.

3.6 Image capture July 2021 © Google.
3.7 City of Norfolk, Virginia.
3.8 U.S. Environmental Protection Administration.

4 Enhancing public open spaces

4.1 Imagery © 2022 Google, Imagery © 2022 CNES, Airbus, Maxar
        Technologies. Map data © 2022 Nashville Davidson County.
4.2 Image Capture February 2021 © 2022 Google.
4.3 photo by vincent desjardins used under Creative Commons
        License 2.0.
4.4 © Google 2022 Image Capture October 2019.
4.5 © Google 2022 Image from 1997.
4.6 Imagery © 2022 Google, Imagery © 2022 CNES, Airbus, Maxar
        Technologies, U.S. Geological Survey, USDA/FPAC/GEO Map
        data © 2022.
4.7 Image Capture June 2019, ©2022 Google.
4.8 Image Capture June 2019, ©2022 Google.

5 Preserving existing urban designs

5.1 Image adapted from a drawing, made in 1903, is from
        Civic Art by Werner Hegemann and Elbert Peets, the
        Architectural Book Publishing Co., 1922. The drawing is in
        the public domain.
5.2 Image capture, September 2021 © 2022 Google.
5.3 Cleveland City Planning Commission.
5.4 Imagery © 2022 Google, © 2022 CNES/Airbus, Maxar
        Technologies, Sanborn, USDA/FRAC/GEO © 2022.
5.5 Imagery © 2022 Google, © 2022 CNES/Airbus, Maxar
        Technologies, Sanborn, USDA/FRAC/GEO © 2022.
5.6 Image capture, July 2021 © 2022 Google.
5.7 Image capture, June 2021 © 2022 Google.

6 Changing regulations to prevent suburban sprawl

6.1 Photo by Maryanne E. Simmons 1995, City of Wildwood.
6.2 Conceptual land use map from the City of Wildwood
        Master Plan.
6.3 Town Center Plan courtesy DPZ CoDesign.
6.4 Image Capture May 2022 © 2022 Google.
6.5 Image Capture May 2022 © 2022 Google.
6.6 Image Capture May 2022 © 2022 Google.

7 Reinventing suburban development

7.1 Imagery © Google, Imagery © Maxar Technologies, U.S.
        Geological Survey, USDA/FPAC/GEO, Map Data © 2022.
7.2 Image Capture June 2022 © 2002 Google.
7.3 Image Capture June 2019 © 2022 Google.

8 Using bus rapid transit in suburbs

8.1 Map by Sasaki, used by permission.
8.2 Diagram by Peter Calthorpe, used by permission.
8.3 Diagram from the New York Regional Plan, 1929, used by permission.
8.4 Diagram used by permission of DPZ CoDesign.
8.5 Graphics by Freedman Tung + Sasaki from "Restructuring the Commercial Strip: A Practical Guide for Planning the Revitalization of Deteriorating Strip Corridors." Development of a Nationally Replicable Approach to Smart Growth Corridor Redevelopment, for the United States Environmental Protection Agency, Washington, DC: 2010.
8.6 Graphics by Freedman Tung + Sasaki from "Restructuring the Commercial Strip: A Practical Guide for Planning the Revitalization of Deteriorating Strip Corridors." Development of a Nationally Replicable Approach to Smart Growth Corridor Redevelopment, for the United States Environmental Protection Agency, Washington, DC: 2010.
8.7 Imagery © Google, Imagery © 2022 CNES/Airbus, Maxar Technologies, U.S. Geological Survey, USDA/FPAC/GEO, Map data © 2022.
8.8 Image capture, Sep 2022 © 2022 Google.
8.9 Photo by Raymond Wambsgans, used according to the Creative Commons Attribution 2.0 generic license.

9 Mobilizing support to redesign an entire city

9.1 Courtesy of WRT.
9.2 Drawing by Yan Wang, courtesy WRT.
9.3 Courtesy WRT.
9.4 Courtesy WRT.
9.5 Courtesy WRT.
9.6 Courtesy WRT.

10 Designing for regions and megaregions

10.1 Courtesy of the Weitzman School of Design at the University of Pennsylvania.
10.2 Courtesy of the Weitzman School of Design at the University of Pennsylvania.
10.3 Courtesy of the Weitzman School of Design at the University of Pennsylvania.
10.4 Courtesy of the Weitzman School of Design at the University of Pennsylvania.
10.5 Courtesy of the Weitzman School of Design at the University of Pennsylvania.

Notes

1 Including the Community in Design Decisions

1 Jonathan Barnett, "A New Planning Process with Built-in Political Support," *Architectural Record,* May, 1966.
2 Jonathan Barnett, *Urban Design as Public Policy: Practical Methods for Improving Cities* (New York: Architectural Record Books, McGraw Hill, 1974).
3 Paul Davidoff, "Advocacy and Pluralism in Planning," *Journal of the American Institute of Planners* 31, no. 4 (1965): 331–338.
4 Michael Adlerstein went on to manage many other projects for the Park Service, was a Vice President of the New York Botanical Garden, and then became an Assistant Secretary General at the United Nations, in charge of the renovation plans for its New York headquarters.
5 The Comprehensive Plan for Wards Corner can be seen at https://docslib. org/doc/5434509/greater-wards-corner-comprehensive-plan.

2 Protecting the Environment

1 Ian McHarg, *Design with Nature* (New York: American Natural History Press, 1969) and subsequent editions.
2 New York City Department of City Planning, *Standards for Planned Unit Development*, 1968. The project on Staten Island is described in Jonathan Barnett, *Urban Design as Public Policy* (McGraw Hill, 1974), pp. 37–39. The drawings on page 38 of this book are from the *Standards for Planned Unit Development*.
3 William H. Whyte, *The Last Landscape* (Garden City, NY: Doubleday, 1968). The quotation appears on page 252 of the 1970 Anchor Books edition.
4 Lane Kendig, with Susan Connor, Cranston Byrd, and Judy Heyman, *Performance Zoning* (Washington, DC, and Chicago, IL: Planners Press, American Planning Association, 1980).
5 Jonathan Barnett, *The Fractured Metropolis, Improving the New City, Restoring the Old City, Reshaping the Region,* Icon Editions (New York: HarperCollins, 1995), pp. 60–65.
6 Susan Hodara, "Irvington, N.Y.: A Walkable Village With Striking Manhattan Views," *New York Times*, August 1, 2018. From the article: "Although Irvington is dotted with multimillion-dollar mansions, its roughly 6,500 residents are a socioeconomically diverse mix."
7 The Irvington Zoning Code is available online. To read the provisions of Article XV, go to https://ecode360.com/11801377.
8 Irvington Environmental Action Plan, https://www.irvingtonny.gov/400/Environmental-Action-Plan.
9 Jonathan Barnett and Brian W. Blaesser, *Reinventing Development Regulations* (Cambridge, MA: Lincoln Institute of Land Policy, 2017).

3 Designing Cities without Designing Buildings

1 I also used this phrase as a chapter heading in my *Urban Design as Public Policy: Practical Methods for Improving Cities,* which described the work of urban designers during John Lindsay's mayoral administration, as cited in Chapter 1.
2 For a more extended discussion of design requirements and their legal basis, please see Chapter 6, "Establishing Design Principles for Public Buildings and Spaces," in *Reinventing Development Regulations* by Jonathan Barnett and Brian W. Blaesser (Cambridge, MA: Lincoln Institute of Land Policy, 2017).

4 Enhancing Public Open Spaces

1 The last names of the original partners of CH2M began with C, H, H, and M. Hill was added to the name later, after a merger. Logically, the firm could have been called CH3M. In any case, the firm has since been merged into Jacobs Engineering and no longer has an independent identity.
2 See the Milwaukee Department of City Development's Regulation and Funding Policy for the RiverWalk: https://city.milwaukee.gov/DCD/Projects/RiverWalk/Regulation–Funding-Policy.

5 Preserving Existing Urban Designs

1 Cleveland's Publc Square has since been redesigned and Superior Avenue within the Square landscaped and narrowed to two lanes.
2 I published two of these maps in my book, *The Fractured Metropolis* (New York: Icon Editions, HarperCollins, 1995), pp. 198, 199 and 202, 203.
3 I published a drawing of the façade for the Society Bank Corporation in *The Fractured Metropolis,* cited above, on page 200.
4 I published an article about some of what was happening in downtown Cleveland in an article, "In Cleveland, of All Places: Urban Rebirth, Complete with Stararchitecture," *Architecture,* December, 1988, pp. 88–89. The title was supplied by Donald Canty, the editor of the magazine.
5 Evan Connell gives a satirical picture of upper-middle-class life in the Country Club district in his two novels: *Mrs. Bridge* and *Mr. Bridge.* These novels were later made into a film by Merchant Ivory with a happy ending totally out of keeping with the books.
6 "Former J.C. Nichols CEO Gets Five Years' Probation," *Kansas City Business Journal,* February 28, 2002. See also "A Family Album of Intrigue; Kansas City Tale of Inside Deals and Outside Investors," by Barnaby J. Feder, *N.Y. Times,* January 1:, 1996.
7 Lisa Rodriguez, "Kansas City Council Approves 'Plaza Bowl' Rules to Keep Short Buildings in the Center," transcript of a broadcast on KCUR, February 14, 2019.

6 Changing Regulations to Prevent Suburban Sprawl

1 I wrote an earlier, and less complete account of planning for Wildwood, "How Wildwood Took Hold of Its Future," *Planning,* Vol. 64, November 1998: 15–17.
2 Wildwood's population in 2020 was estimated to be 35,397.

7 Reinventing Suburban Development

1 See Steve Bailey, "Charleston's Annexation Wars Are Over – The Suburbs Won," *Charleston Post and Courier*, April 7, 2018. Updated September 14, 2020.
2 South Carolina Legislative Audit Council, *Issues Involved in the State Ports Authority's Expansion Plans*, March, 2002, available at https://dc.statelibrary.sc.gov/bitstream/handle/10827/2356/LAC_Issues_Involved_in_the_SPA%27s_Expansion_Plans_2002_Summary.pdf?sequence=5&isAllowed=y.
3 See Jonathan Barnett, "Accidental Cities or New Urban Centers," in *The Fractured Metropolis: Improving the New City, Restoring the Old City, Reshaping the Region* (New York: Harper Collins, 1995), pp. 17–46.
4 Elizabeth Bush, "Daniel Island Scores Another Good Report Card after Irma, But Why?" *The Daniel Island News*, 09/20/2017.
5 I wrote an earlier and much less complete account of planning Daniel Island, published as "Charleston Annex," *Urban Land*, Vol. 66, August, 2007: 100–103.

8 Using Bus Rapid Transit in Suburbs

1 The invention of Bus Rapid Transit should probably be credited to Arthur Ling, the distinguished architect and planner who included an express bus system on separate rights of way in the master plan for Runcorn New Town in the U.K. This transit began operation in 1971. Mayor Jaime Lerner of Curitiba in Brazil, also an architect and planner, deserves the credit for seeing the possibilities of Bus Rapid Transit and deploying it successfully across an entire major city, beginning in 1974.
2 According to an article by Grant Segall in the *Cleveland Plain Dealer*, November 4, 2018 https://www.cleveland.com/news/erry-2018/11/149927818e3851/rta-says-healthline-had-10year.html.
3 Douglas Kelbaugh, editor, *The Pedestrian Pocket Book: A New Suburban Design Strategy*, Princeton Architectural Press, in association with the University of Washington, 1989.
4 Peter Calthorpe, *The Next American Metropolis, Ecology, Community, and the American Dream* (New York: Princeton Architectural Press, 1993).
5 Clarence Perry, "The Neighborhood Unit," in *Regional Survey of New York and Its Environs, Volume VII, Neighborhood and Community Planning* (New York: Regional Plan of New York and Its Environs, 1929).
6 Much more information about these walkable neighborhoods is available on the projects tab of the website DPZ CoDesign https://www.dpz.com/projects/.
7 Michael D. Beyard and Michael Pawlukiewicz, *Ten principles for Reinventing America's Suburban Strips* (Washington, DC: Urban Land Institute, January 2001).
8 ICF International and Freedman Tung & Sasaki, *Restructuring the Commercial Strip: A Practical Guide for Planning the Revitalization of Deteriorating Strip Corridors*, United States Environmental Protection Agency, 2010.
9 Jonathan Barnett and Brian W. Blaesser, *Reinventing Development Regulations* (Cambridge, MA: Lincoln Institute of Land Policy, 2017).
10 BRW had been acquired by another firm, Dames & Moore in 1996, which merged into URS, in 1999, which, in turn, merged into AECOM in 2014.

NOTES

9 Mobilizing Support to Redesign an Entire City

1 The Urban Design Element of the Omaha Master Plan can be read on-line: https://urbanplanning.cityofomaha.org/images/Urban_Design_Element_102720.pdf.

2 The urban design amendments to Omaha's zoning can also be read on-line: https://library.municode.com/ne/omaha/codes/code_of_ordinances?nodeId=OMMUCOCHGEORVOII_CH55ZO_ARTXXIIURDE.

3 I published an account of the Omaha by Design planning process in *Harvard Design Magazine* before the implementation phase was finished. "Omaha by Design – All of It, New Prospects in Urban Planning and Design," *Harvard Design Magazine*, Spring/Summer 2005.

10 Designing for Regions and Megaregions

1 Jan Gottmann, *Megalopolis, The Urbanized Northeastern Seaboard of the United States* (Cambridge, MA, and London, England: MIT Press, 1961).

2 Robert D. Yaro, Ming Zhang, Frederick R. Steiner, *Megaregions and America's Future* (Cambridge, MA: Lincoln Institute of Land Policy, 2022).

3 Thanks to Eugenie Birch, then the chair of the University of Pennsylvania's City Planning Department, who introduced us to each other.

4 Cate Brandt, Andrew Dobshinsky, Ilse Frank, Brad Goetz, Kathleen Grady, Thalia Hussein, Kunbok Lee, Sarah Lovell, Herman Mao, Lauren Mosler, Andrew Nothstine, Abhay Pawar, Tyler Pollesch, Doug Robbins, Jade Shipman, *Alternative Futures for the Seven County Orland Region 2005 – 2050* (City Planning Urban Design Studio 702, The University of Pennsylvania, 2005).

5 Beverly Choi, Alan Cunningham, Melissa Dickens, Jennifer Driver, Lokkay Fan, Jaimie Garcia, Nicole Gibson, Jennie Graves, Mollie Henkel, Shekoofah Khedri, Jennifer Lai, Jason Lally (the mastermind of the ideal conservation network), Marie Lewis, Lori Massa, Alexis Meluski, Laura Ottoson, *An Alternative Future, Florida in the 21st Century, 2020, 2040, 2060* (City Planning Urban Design Studio 702, The University of Pennsylvania, 2007).

6 Crist became an ndependent in 2010 and a Democrat in 2012.

7 Yemi Adediji, Jing Cai, Christian Gass, Angela He, Liyuan Huang, Lou Huang, Dae Hyun Kang, Marta Mackiewicz, Nelson Peng, Steve Scott, Cara Seabury, Gretchen Sweeney, Keiko Vuong, Tya Winn, Fiona Zhu, *Connecting for Global Competitiveness, the Florida Super Region* (City Planning Urban Design Studio 702, The University of Pennsylvania, Spring, 2010), https://issuu.com/pennplanning/docs/florida_super_region.

Index

Note: *Italicised* page numbers refer to figures in the text.

acquisition of environmentally sensitive land 145; of building sites 4; minimizing disruption by city 4; controversial 39; costs 141
Adlerstein, Michael 12
advocacy planning 10–11
Alschuler, John 94, 95, 101
Amundsen, Craig 114
appropriateness in historic district 48
ArcGIS Spatial Analyst computer program 140
Architectural Record, article Downtown Cincinnati 4
Architectural Review Board in Wildwood, Missouri 46
Arizona Sun Corridor megaregion 133
Art Commission, Cleveland 71
Article XV, Resource Protection, Village of Irvington zoning 28
A. T. & T. Building in New York City 40

Bacon, Edmund 22, 23, 29
Barnes, Edward Larrabee 4
Barnett, Jonathan: *Designing the Megaregion, Meeting Urban Challenges at a New Scale* 146; *The Fractured Metropolis* 25, 96; *Managing the Climate Crisis* 146; *Reinventing Development Regulations* 28, 32, 113; *Urban Design as Public Policy: Practical Methods for Improving Cities* 10
Basin and Range megaregion 133, 134
Beckley, Robert. 60
Bedford Stuyvesant Renewal and Rehabilitation Corporation 11
Blaesser, Brian W. 80–81, 84, 119, 130; *Reinventing Development Regulations* 28, 32, 113

Blight Means Somebody Else Wants Your Building 39
Board of Architectural Review, Charleston, SC 45
Bouw, Matthijs: *Managing the Climate Crisis* 146
Bronx Park *8*, 9
Brumley, Frank W. 101
Brunner, Arnold 65, *66*
Brush Creek, Kansas City 76–77
build-to lines 27, 46, 47, 67, 78, 126, 127
Bunnell, Mark 45
Bunster, Ignacio 52
Burgee, John 40, *43*
Burnham, Daniel 65, *66*, 67
Bus Rapid Transit 105–117, *106–107*, *115*; in commercial corridors 110–114; Cleveland Health Line 114–115; transit-based development in suburbs 108–109; urban design strategies 116–117; walkable destinations 110
Byrd, Warren 94

Calthorpe, Peter 108; *The Next American Metropolis, Ecology, Community, and the American Dream* 108, *109*
Carrère, John 65, *66*
Cascadia megaregion 134
Central Plains megaregion 133
CH2MHill 58
Chapin, Linda 135, 137, 139, 142
Charleston, SC Board of Architectural Review 45, see also Daniel Island
Cincinnati process for agreeing on an urban design plan, 4 – 5

INDEX

City Beautiful Movement 65
city design without designing
buildings 34–51; design
guidelines in property transaction
37–42; design review 42–48;
implementation strategies 50–51;
Lincoln Square 35–37; streetscape
designs 48–50; in zoning districts
35–37
City of New York conventional
street plan for Arden Heights site
(Staten Island) 21
City of New York P anned Unit
Development zoning 23
city comprehensive redesign
118–132; Omaha 121–132, 122, 125
Civic Place Districts 132
civic urban design 2
Clas, Alfred 55
Cleveland, Ohio: City Planning
Department 70; Regional Transit
Authority 115
Cleveland Art Commission 71
Cleveland Group Plan 65–73, 66
Cleveland Health Line 105, 107;
design of 114–115
Cleveland Public Auditorium 65
Cleveland Public Library 71
climate changes 143–144
commercial corridors, Bus Rapid
Transit for 110–114
community-based plans as guide for
future development 15
community participation in planning
and design decisions 2, 3–18; in
charrettes 13–15, 17, 84, 86, 86,
88–89,
implementation strategies 17–18;
rejection of 11–13; in urban
renewal in the Bronx 6–10,
in working committees 15, in
workshops 13, 14
community urban design 2
Congrès internationaux
d'architecture moderne (CIAM) 34
Congressional legislation on urban
national parks 11
Convention Center 71–72
Cooper, Alexander 37
Cope Linder Architects 61, 62
Country Club Plaza District in Kansas
City 73, 75–78, 76, 77
COVID-19 37, 110
Crist, Charlie 142

Crow Holdings 101
Cullinane, Sue. 82
Cumberland River in Nashville 55

Daniel Island, Charleston, SC 93–103;
highway interchange design
95–97, 98; implementing the plan
101; natural setting and rising
seas 97; neighborhoods of 97–102;
residential neighborhoods 99;
town and community centers
102–103; Town Center 99–100
Daniel Island Club 101
Davidoff, Paul 10, 11
Davidson County Courthouse,
Nashville 52
*Designing the Megaregion, Meeting
Urban Challenges at a New Scale*
(Barnett) 146
design review 42–48; boards 46;
build-to lines 47; conformity
to historic styles 48; criteria
46–48; height limits 46–47; in
historic districts 45–46; location
and masking of services 47;
by planning departments
44–45; setbacks 46; transparency
requirements 47
Design with Nature (McHarg) 19, 20
design workshops 13
Destination Midtown (Omaha) 61, 63
development regulations 19, 34, 84,
150; changes 146; comprehensive
plan 92; environmentally based
148; height limit 46–47;
St. Louis County 83; zoning and
subdivision ordinances 134;
see also regulations
Dierberg's Markets 88–89, 89
Dobshinsky, Andrew 135, 137
Dougherty, James 141
Dover, Victor 141
Downtown Development Strategy
(Pittsburgh) 45
Downtown Streetscape Handbook
(Norfolk Virginia) 49
DPZ CoDesign 84
Drury Plaza Hotel, Cleveland 69
Duany, Andrés 14, 46, 47, 84, 88,
110, 112, 129

Eckstut, Stanton 37
Elliott, Donald H 4, 5, 10, 11
Emanuel, Manuel S. 25

environment, protection of 19–51; environmental designs into regulations 28–32; implementation strategies 32–33; natural environment 24–28; park plans 19–24; planned development 19–24; regulation 24–28

environmental designs translated into regulations 28–32

environmental impact statements 12–13

Faga, Barbara 141
Fahey, Mike 119, 129
Farmer, Paul 44
Fazio, Tom 101
Federal Reserve Building 71
Flatow, Eugenia 5
Florida 133, 134–144, *138–140*; Bureau of Economic and Business Research 135; changing plans for development 143–144; environmental sensitivity in *140*; Seven County Orlando Region 134, GeoPlan *145*; Tampa/Orlando super region 142–143
Floyd Bennett Field in Brooklyn, New York City 11
Forbes Avenue in Pittsburgh 42
Fort Hancock 12–13
The Fractured Metropolis (Barnett) 25, 96
Fraim, Paul, 16
Freedman Tung + Sasaki 113, *113*
Front Range megaregion 133

Gateway National Recreation Area 11, 12
geographic information systems (GIS) 135, 137; map 29; Orlando, Florida 138, *138*
Golden Gate National Recreation Area 11
Gorman, Anita 75
Gottmann, Jean: *Megalopolis* 133
Gottschalk, John 118
government intervention 2
government-subsidized housing *8*, 59
Greater Milwaukee Committee 58
Greater Wards Corner Area Comprehensive Plan 15
green parking lots 31–32

green urban design 2
Greystar Capital Partners 101
Guggenheim, Harry Frank 94

Haines Lundberg and Waehler (HLW) 4
Hammer, David 82, 83, 84, 91
Hansen, Judy 75
Hawkins Partners 54
Heath, Ellen 141
height limits 46
Heiskell, Marian 11
Henrichsen, Linda 67
Hickel, Walter 11
highway interchange, Daniel Island 95, *98*
Hirons, Frederic Charles 52
Holzman, Malcolm 71, 72
Housing Act of 1954 4
Houston 133

implementation strategies 64; city design 50–51; environment, protection of 32–33; suburban development 103–104; reducing suburban sprawl 91–92; urban designs, preservation of 78
interchange design, Daniel Island 95–97
Irvington, New York: development in *26*; environmental zoning 25–28

Jackson, Tim 141
Jaffe, Norman 22, 23
J.C. Nichols Company 75, 77
J. M. Kaplan Fund 4
Johnson, Philip 40, 41, *43*
Johnson, Tom L. 65
Jones, Rees 101
Journal of the American Institute of Planners 10

Kansas City Redevelopment Authority 73
Kansas City, Country Club Plaza Urban Design and Development Plan 73–78
Kelbaugh, Douglas: *The Pedestrian Pocket Book: A New Suburban Design Strategy* 108
Kendig, Lane 24, 28; *Performance Zoning* 25
Kennedy, Robert 11
Key Bank Corporation 71

INDEX

Key Tower 71, 74
Khoury, Marina 46
Klavon Design Associates *43*
Kulash, Walter 82

Lake Erie 65
Laney, John 73
The Last Landscape (Whyte) 23
Lauritzen, Bruce 118
L'Ecole des Beaux Arts in Paris 13
Lennertz, Bill 14–15
Lickerman, Stephanie 82
Lincoln Center for the Performing
  Arts 36
Lincoln Square Special Zoning
  District 35–37, *38–39*
Lindsay, John 3, 4, 10, 11
Lively Omaha 118–119
location and masking of services 47
Logue, Edward 6
Low, Tom 86–87
Lurcott, Robert 44

Managing the Climate Crisis (Barnett
  and Bouw) 146
Manning, David 53
Marcus, Norman 21, 35
Mark Clark Expressway 94, 95, 96
Marriott Hotel 69
Marston, Gerald 141
McCarthy, Lynn 77
McHarg, Ian: *Design with Nature*
  19, 20
Megalopolis (Gottmann) 133
megaregions *see* regions and
  megaregions
Meier, Richard 6, *8*, 9
Metro Nashville Park 52
Micale, Nando 120
Midtown Crossing 61, *62*
Midtown Omaha 60–63
Midwest 133
Milwaukee River 58
Milwaukee RiverWalk 55–60,
  59–60
Model Cities Program (New York
  City) 5, 17
Molloy, Thomas 52
Moore, James 141
Morrison, Hunter 65, 114
Moses, Robert 3
Mumford, Lewis 95
Mutual of Omaha 60–61, *61–62*, 63
Myers, Sherrill 58

Nashville Civic Design Center: *Plan
  of Nashville* 55
Nashville Metro Government City
  Hall 52
Nashville Public Square 52–55, *54*
National Park Service 11–13
National Seashore concept 11
natural environment, protection of
  24–28
Neighborhood Alliances in
  Omaha 129
New Jersey: Gateway National
  Recreation Area 11, 12; Sandy
  Hook 12
New York City 4, 35; A. T. &
  T. Building 40; five boroughs 20,
  20; Gateway National Recreation
  Area 11, 12; Model Cities Program
  5, 17; Planned Unit Development
  23; conventional street plan *21*;
  zoning law history 34
New York City Housing Authority 7
New York City Planning Department
  19, *22*, 34
New York City Zoning Resolution,
  planned unit development
  amendment 21 – 23, *23*, special
  zoning districts 35
New York State: Robert Moses
  policies 3; Urban Development
  Corporation (UDC) 6
*The Next American Metropolis,
  Ecology, Community, and the
  American Dream* (Calthorpe)
  108, *109*
Nixon, Richard 11
Nixon administration 11
Norfolk, Virginia: Downtown
  Streetscape Handbook *49*; Wards
  Corner district 16
Norquist, John 58
Northeast 133
Northern California 134
numerical site grading standards
  30–31

Omaha, Nebraska 121–132, *122*, *125*;
  areas of civic importance 124–127;
  design standards for annexation
  127–129; master plan *128*, *130*,
  132; midtown 80, neighborhoods
  129–130; strategies 130–132
Omaha Community Foundation 119
Omaha World Herald 120, 131

open spaces *see* public open spaces
Otis, Lauren 37

Panel Advisory Services by Urban
  Land Institute 15
parking lots 31–32, 52, 61, *61*, 64, 75,
  79, *89*, 96, 102, *107*, 121, 127, 132
park plans, environment protection
  by 19–24
Pasanella, Giovanni 3, 4, 6, 7, 9
*The Pedestrian Pocket Book: A
  New Suburban Design Strategy*
  (Kelbaugh) 108
Pelli, Cesar 67, 71
Performance Zoning (Kendig) 25
Perry, Clarence 109; neighborhood
  diagram *111*, Perry's
  neighborhood diagram revised by
  Andrés Duany, Elizabeth Plater-
  Zyberk *114*
Peters, Robert 119, 120
Peterson, Steven 25, *26*, 28
Philadelphia Planning
  Commission 23
Piedmont-Atlantic megaregion 133
planned development, environment
  protection by 19–24
planned unit development (PUD) 21,
  22, *24*, 24–25, 30
Planning Agencies 44
planning and design, community
  involvement in 10–17; advocacy
  and pluralism in 10–11
Planning Commission 34, 35
planning workshops 13
Plan of Nashville 55
Plater-Zyberk, Elizabeth 14, 84, 94,
  110, *112*, 129, 141
pluralism in planning 10–11
Polshek, James 6
PPG Industries (Pittsburgh Plate
  Glass) 38, 39, 40, 42, *43–44*
Prentice Chan Ohlhausen 6, 7, 9
property transaction, design
  guidelines in 37–42
public hearing 5, 30; far too late to
  show a community a plan for its
  future 3
public open spaces 52–64;
  implementation strategies
  64; Midtown Omaha 60–63;
  Milwaukee RiverWalk 55–60;
  Nashville Public Square 52–55, *54*
Purcell, Bill 52, 55

rain garden *50*
Redevelopment Authority 38
redesign *see* city redesign
Regional Plan Association 11
*Regional Plan for New York City and
  Its Environs* (Perry) *111*
regions and megaregions 133–146;
  Florida 134–144, *138–140*; urban
  design strategies 144–146;
  see also suburban sprawl
regulations: environment,
  protection of 24–28;
  environmental designs into
  28–32; *see also* development
  regulations
*Reinventing Development
  Regulations* (Barnett and Blaesser)
  28, 32, 113
Resource Protection, in the Village
  of Irvington's zoning 28
Rettie, Dwight 12
Riley, Joseph P. Jr. 46, 93
River Landing Drive 96–97
Robertson, Jaquelin 3, 4, 10, 94
Rockaway Peninsula 12
Rogers, Archibald 4

same-sized lot requirement 29–30
Sandy Hook, New Jersey 12
San Francisco, California: Golden
  Gate National Recreation
  Area 11
Schiffman, Ronald 10
Schmitt, Chris 102
Scott, Rick 143
setbacks 46, 47, 50, 127
Shea, Brian 97
shopping centers 16–17
Sloan, Matthew 101, 102
Smythe, Henry 94
Society Bank Corporation 67, 71
Sohio Building, Cleveland, Ohio *68*
solar access 32
South Carolina Coastal Council 97
South Carolina State Ports
  Authority 95
Southern Boulevard, Bronx,
  New York City *8*
Southern California megaregion 134
Special Theater Zoning District 35
special zoning districts 46–48, 51
Spellman, Connie 118, 120, 132
Staten Island 24
Stinson, Ken 118

INDEX

165

Stokes Building extension of Cleveland Central Library 71
stormwater *50*; retention measures 31
streetscape designs 48–50
subdivision: laws 19; ordinance 30–31; zoning and 24, 33, 34
suburban development 93–104; at Daniel Island 93–103; implementation strategies 103–104
suburban sprawl 79–92; implementation strategies to prevent 91–92; Wildwood 79–91
SunRail 142–143
Swiss, Fred 44

Tacchi, Dennis 82
Tampa/Orlando Super Region 142
Terwilliger, J. Ronald 101
Texas Triangle megargeion 133
Tiebout Avenue Bronx New York City 6–7, *7*
Town Center, Daniel Island *99–100*, 102–103; Wildwood MO 88–91, *89–90*
transit-oriented development (TOD) 109
transparency requirements 47
Travers, Warren 96
Tuck-Hinton 54
Twin Parks Plan 4–6; eastern side of *8*; western edge of *6*

United States zoning in 19; urban renewal 3
University Heights, Bronx, New York 5, 6, *6*, 9
Urban, James 48, 49
urban design, conditions for effective implementation 1–2, in a changing climate147–148
Urban Design as Public Policy: Practical Methods for Improving Cities (Barnett) 10
Urban Design Element of Omaha Master Plan 131, 132
Urban Design Group 22
Urban Design Review Board for Omaha, Nebraska 46
urban designs, preservation of 65–78; Brush Creek 76–77; Cleveland Group Plan 65–73, *66*; Country Club Plaza District

in Kansas City 73, 75–78; implementation strategies 78
urban heat islands 31
U.S. Army Corps of Urban Land Institute (ULI) 110, 111, 112, 114; Panel Advisory Services 15
Urban Redevelopment Authority of Pittsburgh 37–38
urban renewal changes needed 3, 4–10
U.S. Army unexploded ordinance at Fort Hancock, Gateway National Recreation Area 13
Engineers, redesign for Brush Creek 77
U.S. Environmental Protection Agency 112–114, *113*

Village Greens, Staten Island, N.Y.C. 24
Vogel, Daniel 81, 84
Voinovich, George 66
Vujnich, Joe 84, 91, 92

walkable destinations, Bus Rapid Transit 110
Walker Parking Consultants 53
Wallace Roberts and Todd (WRT) 52–53, *54*, *55*, 119–120, 141
Wards Corner 15, 17; future development *16*
Weber, Del 119
Webster Avenue, Bronx, N.Y. 6, 6–7, 9
Weinstein, Richard 3, 4, 10, 11, 12
Weintraub, Myles 3, 4, 10
Westin Element Hotel 61
Whyte, William H.: *The Last Landscape* 23
Wildwood, Missouri 79–91; design concepts 82–84; erosion *80*; master plan 82–84, *85*; New Downtown 84–88; regulations 84; rejection of suburban growth 79–82; Town Center Plan 88–91, *89–90*
wind access 32
working committee of local citizens 15

Zicarelli, Mario 5, 6
Zoning as powerful urban design tool 34, billiard table approach to *27*, 28; blind to natural

environment, treats land as commodity 19,; criteria for design incorporated in 47, plan as basis for 103; for solar and wind access 32,; GIS added to official map 29; and site plan review, 44, 45; revisions to implement environmental preservation 33, 34, street plan and 22; subdivision and 24, using creatively 50–51 zoning district for Lincoln Square, N.Y.C. 35–37